A SLOBBERING LOVE AFFAIR

A SLOBBERING LOVE AFFAIR

The True (and Pathetic) Story of the Torrid Romance Between Barack Obama and the Mainstream Media

BY BERNARD GOLDBERG

Since 1947
REGNERY
PUBLISHING, INC.
An Eagle Publishing Company • Washington, DC

Cataloging-in-Publication data on file with the Library of Congress
ISBN 978-1-59698-090-7

Published in the United States by
Regnery Publishing, Inc.
One Massachusetts Avenue, NW
Washington, DC 20001
www.regnery.com

Manufactured in the United States of America

10 9 8 7 6 5 4 3 2 1

Books are available in quantity for promotional or premium use. Write to Director of Special Sales, Regnery Publishing, Inc., One Massachusetts Avenue NW, Washington, DC 20001, for information on discounts and terms or call (202) 216-0600.

FOR NANCY, BRIAN, AND CATHERINE

CONTENTS

INTRODUCTION

A few years ago I spoke by phone to a graduate class in politics at American University in Washington, D.C., about my then new book, *Bias*, which was an insider's account of how liberal journalists operate in the so-called mainstream media. I had been a correspondent with CBS News for twenty-eight years and so I knew how and why supposedly fair-minded journalists slanted the news to fit their own worldview. *Bias* had become a *New York Times* number one bestseller and was creating a lot of buzz, and not just among conservatives. Liberals were talking about the book too, but not in a good way.

My former colleagues at CBS News, as you might imagine, were not happy with *Bias*, and one even told Howard Kurtz of the *Washington Post* that writing it "was an act of treason." And that was one of the nicer things that liberals in the media said about me. *Washington Post* TV critic Tom Shales reached deep into his bag of clichés and called me a "no-talent hack." Columnist Michael Kinsley was much kinder; he only said I was "dense." And when my good friend Jed Duvall, who was a former CBS News correspondent, ran into a Washington journalist we both had worked with at CBS (I'll call him Marty, which just happens to be his real name) and asked if he had read my book, Marty simply declared, "That bastard!" "Did you read Bernie's book," Jed asked again. "That bastard," Marty repeated like a clever parrot that had just learned a new phrase. Turns out, he had not read the book and said he had no intention of reading it, but Marty was sure of one thing: I was a bastard.

The kids at American University did read the book since it was part of a class assignment. After I talked about *Bias* on the speakerphone for fifteen or twenty minutes and asked for questions or comments, one young woman said all she wanted to do after she read the book was throw it across the room. "Very liberal," I thought. The other students were more reasonable, but none had anything good to say about *Bias*. Having already been accused of treason and been called a no-talent hack, dense, and a bastard, this was no big deal.

Then the professor jumped in. "Isn't it the role of the media to effect change in society?"

It was a statement posing as a question.

"Your change or mine?" I asked.

Silence. After a while, I thought that I had either gone deaf or that the phone went dead.

It had never occurred to this supposedly well-educated liberal man who taught liberal kids at a liberal college that change comes in more than one package. My change, I explained to him, would be very different from his. I didn't go into a lot of detail that day, but so you know, the kind of change that I want includes lower taxes and smaller government. I want an end to affirmative action, at least the way it's currently practiced. In a post-September 11 world, I want ethnic profiling at our airports. And I want kids on college campuses who shout down speakers they don't agree with tossed out of the auditorium, then out of school, either temporarily or permanently.

This, obviously, was not the kind of change the good professor had in mind. The change he wanted the media to effect was liberal change, the only change worth effecting as far as liberals are concerned.

My point is this: it is not the media's role to effect change—either the professor's kind *or* mine. And while we're on the subject, it is not the media's role to comfort the afflicted and afflict the comfortable, even though this is taken as gospel in America's liberal newsrooms. It is the media's role to report the news, not to advocate for causes, no matter how noble journalists think the cause might be.

• • •

Then the presidential campaign of 2008 came along and that long-ago exchange with the professor came rushing back to me.

Never in my memory were so many journalists so intent on effecting change as they were during the campaign of 2008. Sure, mainstream journalists always root for the Democrat. But this time it was different. This time journalists were not satisfied merely being partisan witnesses to history. This time they wanted to be real players and help determine the outcome. This time they were on a mission—a noble, historic mission, as far as they were concerned. In fact, I could not remember a time when so many supposedly objective reporters had acted so blatantly as full-fledged advocates for one side—and without even a hint of embarrassment.

The media's crush on Barack Obama began even before his presidential campaign. There was just something about the guy—his personal charisma, his liberalism, and of course, the fact that he is black—that made him irresistible to mainstream journalists. As *Politico* editor in chief John Harris recalled about his time with the *Washington Post*, "A couple years ago, you would send a reporter out with Obama, and it was like they needed to go through detox when they came back—'Oh, he's so impressive, he's so charismatic,' and we're kind of like, 'Down, boy.'"

The intensity of this love affair grew exponentially once Obama began running for president. The media not only gave him extremely favorable coverage, but they also took the only other real contender for the nomination, Hillary Clinton, into the back room and beat her with a rubber hose. There was a simple explanation for this: in liberal media circles, race trumps sex. It was more important, as many journalists saw it, that America get its first black president than its first woman president. Or as political pundit Mike Barnicle put it on MSNBC just four days before the election, an Obama victory would represent an "only-in-America tale" that would provide a "a great reflection" of America to the rest of the world.

Translation: we need the black guy to win *because he's black*.

But there was another reason that wasn't as obvious. Helping to elect our first African-American president would make liberal journalists feel better about the most important people in their lives—*themselves*. See, they could say (if not out loud, then certainly in private when they were congratulating themselves on their goodness, in the company of other wonderful journalists), *we* did something about America's ugly racial history. *We* did something this *broken* country can finally be proud of!

After that, it was a no-brainer: Obama vs. McCain? New vs. old? Liberal vs. (sometimes) conservative? Come on! And this time the mainstream media did more than merely spin the news to help the Democrats; this time they *de facto* enlisted in the Obama campaign. And they didn't give a damn what you or anybody else thought about it.

• • •

From very early on, I had no doubt Obama would win. I read the polls like everybody else, but it was much more than that. Here was a mysterious man who came out of nowhere, which was enticing in itself. And he possessed qualities no politician in my lifetime, except maybe John F. Kennedy, had possessed, especially a youthful charisma that made him immensely likeable even if you didn't care much for his politics. Yes, Ronald Reagan was likeable, too. But that was different. Reagan was your grandfather. Obama is your friend.

Sure, sometimes this newcomer with the unusual name came off as too cool for school. And it is certainly true that conservatives who could not get beyond his liberal ideology weren't all that impressed with his million dollar smile. But lots of ordinary Americans who didn't eat, drink, and sleep politics were drawn to Obama in a way they had never been drawn to any of those ordinary, run-of-the mill, vanilla politicians who told us they wanted to be president.

I didn't vote for Obama, but like so many others—supporters and detractors—I was moved by his victory speech on election night, when he spoke so eloquently to that huge crowd at Grant Park in Chicago. That audience knew, and we knew too, that there was something special about this moment in American history.

But when the sun came up the next morning, while most of the media was still swooning from the night before, Joe Scarborough, on his MSNBC show *Morning Joe*, threw a bucket of cold water all over the mainstream media.

"I'll tell you my biggest fear for Barack Obama," Scarborough said. "He has been sainted. He is Saint Barack. The same mainstream media that tried so desperately to get him elected has engaged in hyperbole, engaged in exaggeration. They have *deified* this man while destroying everybody that got in his path."

He was right, of course. And he was right, too, when he noted that the media, by forsaking their role as an honest broker of information, had put their guy, the president-elect, in a potentially tough spot.

"And what they have done for Barack Obama," Joe declared, was that "they have set up such unrealistic expectations that no politician could meet those expectations. I just hope that all of the people who got involved in this election do not become disillusioned when he doesn't reach those lofty heights. The *New York Times* has done more than any other paper, I think—they have done a disservice to Barack Obama because they deified him. We never saw the negative articles from the *Times*. They attacked Cindy McCain viciously, they went after John McCain, but they did not report the Barack Obama story. Americans will find he doesn't walk on water and I'm concerned for him when that happens."

Make no mistake: this is *not* the same old liberal bias we have witnessed for years. In 2008, the mainstream media crossed a line. As a result, their credibility is in tatters. Hardly anyone trusts them anymore. This is not good for them, of course. But it may be even worse for *us*, as we will see.

• • •

This was the year the mainstream media finally jumped the shark. They didn't simply flirt with Obama. They carried on a slobbering love affair with him right out in public.

A journalist I know who helps run a big cable news program told me that for the liberal media, getting Obama elected "was a righteous crusade. It was okay to be biased because the cause was noble."

During his campaign, Obama may indeed have been a man with an air of detachment, that rare politician who always seems to exude coolness. But journalists were anything but cool and detached. They had the passion of the star-struck crowds that came to hear speak, or just to see in person, The One, as Oprah had called him. An NBC News correspondent even admitted that "it's almost hard to remain objective" when covering such a towering presence as Barack Obama.

And much of the media showed very little appetite for stories that might embarrass The One they were rooting for. He told us that in twenty years of going to the Trinity United Church of Christ on Chicago's South Side, he never—not even once—heard his minister say the crazy things we heard on videotape—and the mainstream media refused to press him on it. He said his relationship with a 1970s domestic terrorist was "flimsy"—and the media gladly believed him. He said he had next to nothing to do with ACORN, an organization famous for submitting fraudulent voter registrations for Democrats—and the media bought that, too. And just in case he were to lose somehow, they had an excuse ready for that one as well: "Racism *is the only reason* McCain might beat him" [my emphasis] was the sub-headline over a piece by a prominent liberal writer in *Slate*, the online magazine.

Walter Cronkite once said the press needs to be skeptical so the American people don't become cynical. But skepticism was in short supply in 2008. After all, the media were not gushing over a mere politician. No, this was the man who could atone for America's sins, repair our tarnished image around the world, and in the words of Michelle Obama, "fix our souls." Barack Obama was the Redeemer; the Anointed One, who could heal our wounds.

And while the media were having virtual sex with Obama they ran stories (including on the front page of the *New York Times*) about a supposedly real sexual affair between John McCain and a young, attractive female lobbyist without so much as a shred of evidence that the rumor—passed on by two unnamed sources—was true.

They had more interest in Sarah Palin's wardrobe than they did in Barack Obama's associations and alliances with radicals—from the unhinged Reverend Wright to the bomber Bill Ayers to the Palestinians Obama partied with in Chicago, some of whom called Israelis terrorists and compared them to Osama bin Laden.

When conservatives tried to make an issue of these alliances, the Obama campaign and the mainstream media spoke again with one voice, lecturing us that this was nothing more than McCarthy-style guilt by association. Besides, they said, it was old news, and insignificant old news at that.

No matter how historically important this election was for all Americans—yes, for *all* Americans, whether we supported Obama or not—journalists will pay a hefty price for their dedication to the man who would become president. They may not understand it yet, but they squandered what little credibility they had left—all for their *noble* cause, of course. I don't believe the media got Obama elected, as explained later in this book. However, because of their naked attempt to do so, almost no one outside the Upper West Side of Manhattan or Nancy Pelosi's congressional district in San Francisco believes them anymore.

After Obama won, Dick Morris, the political commentator who used to work for Bill Clinton, told me, "In 2004 the mainstream media did a bad job of being impartial. In 2008, they did a good job of being partial."

But as bad as things were, there's a good chance they're going to get worse. As my friend Rush Limbaugh said to me in an interview, which I'll get to later in this book, Barack Obama is too historically important to fail. The media simply will not let it happen.

In fact, after he won, thanks to a giddy media, we started hearing about a most congenial spot, a magical place America had instantly become—the wonderful land of Bamalot.

That professor at American University must be smiling. All the mainstream media did during the presidential campaign of 2008 was to fulfill their role. All they did was to try to effect change in society.

Their change.

That is what this book is about.

Chapter One

THE MEDIA'S GET OUT
OF JAIL FREE CARD

Conservatives have been up-in-arms for a while now over the unfair treatment their side gets in the media. But during the presidential campaign of 2008 their anger became much more intense. And for good reason.

Let's be honest: we're only human. So no matter how fair we *think* we are, we process information through a filter of our *own* biases. My left-wing friends, for example, hate FOX News and they honestly believe that all you get on FOX News are conservatives—one loudmouth right-winger after another. Never mind that this is delusional. Liberals believe it nonetheless, mainly because of the Windex Effect.

The Windex Effect enables liberals to see right through the liberal commentators on FOX News. Sure, they physically see them and hear them. But liberals don't jump off the screen to my liberal pals. Liberals don't register to them the way conservatives, whose views they detest, register. When my lefty comrades hear liberal opinions on FOX News, they don't even think of them as liberal. They think of them as reasonable, or civil, or simply as middle-of-the-road. But the conservatives on FOX News capture the attention of liberals the way a stink bomb going off in their living room would capture their attention. To them, conservatives are not simply wrong—they are repulsive. Conservative points of view register in their liberal brains in a completely different way.

Conservatives, meanwhile, view the media through their own prism. When I hear an angry, nasty liberal rant on cable television, for instance, it affects me neurologically. I fume. If I hadn't paid a ton of money for my giant flat screen plasma TV, I'd throw my shoe at it. But when I hear someone I agree with, I simply smile calmly and pleasantly nod. The passion is just not there. So to some extent, liberals in the media are right when they say, "Bias is in the eye of the beholder."

The problem is that journalists use this as a handy "get out of jail free" card. They use it to dismiss their critics, to say, "If you think we're biased this proves that you're the one who's really biased." Jim Lehrer, for one, said just that to Stephen Colbert. "Bias is what people who hear or read the news bring to the story, not what the journalist brings to the reporting," he claimed.

Since he was making the point to a comedian, perhaps he was half-kidding—though I doubt it, because journalists really do believe this arrogant nonsense. Tom Brokaw told the *Columbia Journalism Review* that "bias—like beauty—is in the eye of the beholder." What Tom was really saying, for those of you who are not fluent in bull crap, was, "We honest impartial objective fair journalists are not the problem. You right-wing morons—*you're the problem!*"

But self-indulgent journalistic sanctimony can't hide the fact that, quite often, bias really is bias and the guilty party isn't the conservative consumer of news but the liberal journalist who is slanting the news to fit his own ideology.

And in the presidential campaign of 2008 the boys on the media bus drove the vehicle right over the cliff. They voluntarily gave up their role as impartial referee. They decided, either consciously or otherwise, to use the power of the press and TV to accomplish what, in their view, was an important and worthy goal: to get their guy, the *good guy*, elected president of the United States.

Of course, most of them would never admit to any of this. Telling the truth, after all, can get you in trouble. But in fairness, they're not actually lying if they believe their own propaganda. I know these people, I used to work with them, and I can assure you that if you hooked even the most biased reporter up to a lie detector machine, while he was swearing that he was not in the tank for Barack Obama the needle on the polygraph wouldn't budge, not even a little. That doesn't mean he's telling the truth. All it means is that he doesn't have an ounce of introspection. I have met guys working the overnight shift at 7-11 doling out Slurpees and Camels to insomniacs who are more introspective than a lot of journalists I know.

●   ●   ●

If you didn't notice the pro-Obama bias during the campaign, you were either dead or in a coma. If you were dead, there's no reason to continue reading.

Evidence of bias was overwhelming. You couldn't turn on your TV during the campaign without hearing some slobbering reporter refer to Obama as a "rock star." McCain, on the other had, was the old, grumpy, white guy.

I'm not saying that everyone on television or in the press has to abide by the Edward R. Murrow gold standard of reporting (in fact, Murrow himself, in his own way, first blurred the line between news and commentary), but there are limits. Perhaps daytime television should be held to even lower standards, but if so, it certainly lived down to them. On the one hand, there was Oprah Winfrey, who actively campaigned for Obama. To her credit, once the McCain versus Obama race got underway, she played it fairly straight, not having either of the candidates on her show. But even then, one has to wonder why a feminist like Oprah, with her vast audience of women viewers, would not dive into one of the biggest women's interest issues of the campaign and interview Sarah Palin.

That's ignoring a story, a big story, perhaps the biggest story of the campaign for her audience—in fact, a custom-made Oprah story: a mother of five, one child with Down

Syndrome, a son going off to the army, an unwed daughter pregnant; and Palin herself a former beauty queen, current governor of Alaska, and finally a vice presidential candidate. What more could you want; how does an Oprah producer ignore that?

Still, it's not as bad as the true dregs, shows like *The View*, where McCain was treated like a racist despot, with Whoopie Goldberg demanding to know if he planned to throw her back into slavery. Meanwhile, Michelle Obama was feted like Mother Theresa.

More important than daytime television, of course, is the prime time news, the major daily newspapers—the serious stuff. Only this time, by any objective standard, the so-called mainstream media behaved not as serious, responsible journalists, but as seriously committed partisans.

The *New York Times* editorialized that McCain was running a "dismal" and "ugly" campaign.

The *Times* published Obama's op-ed on Iraq, but refused to run one by McCain unless he reworked it to suit the paper's sensibilities.

When Obama went overseas, all three network news anchors tagged along. When McCain went overseas, not one of them showed any interest in going.

Four days after Obama won the Iowa Caucus, NBC News correspondent Lee Cowan, without a hint of embarrassment, said that "it's almost hard to remain objective" when covering Obama because "it's infectious, the energy," when Obama speaks to big crowds.

For its October cover, the *Atlantic* magazine hired a photographer who *intentionally* shot McCain to look like a monster. Turns out she was a self-described "hardcore Democrat." The magazine didn't use the "diabolical McCain" picture on its cover, but it did use one that the photographer didn't bother to touch up. "I left his eyes red and his skin looking bad," she later admitted, adding, "Maybe it was somewhat irresponsible for [the *Atlantic*] to hire me."

You think? Still, some on the Left were arguing that while there indeed was a pro-Obama tilt in the media, it had nothing to do with liberal media bias, which they dismissed as a conservative myth. What was really happening, their argument went, was that Obama was beating McCain in the polls and that perception—of Obama as a winner—was what was driving his favorable news coverage. And while there may be something to that, there was also the *tone* of the coverage, the fawning, *I'm-just-so-thrilled-to-be-in-Obama's-presence* tone—that led many of us inescapably to conclude that a lot of mainstream journalists were not just *covering* Barack Obama, they were *championing* him.

There was *NBC Nightly News* anchor Brian Williams, who showed Obama an issue of *Newsweek* with Obama on the cover and fawningly asked The One, "How does this feel, of all the honors that have come your way, all the publicity?... Who does it make you think of? Is there, is there a loved one?"

There was Jeff Glor, one of the rising stars at CBS News, who reported on "Five Things You Should Know about Barack Obama." Sounding more like Obama's campaign manager than a network news correspondent, Glor helpfully related some really crucial information on the fastest rising star in politics: "In addition to enjoying basketball and

cycling during down time, Obama loves to play Scrab-
ble.... Obama's job as a teenager was at a Baskin-Robbins
and to this day he does not like ice cream.... This is a man
who plays to win. No matter what it is, whether it's the
woman he wants to date or elected office or board games,
there is an ambition there. There is a determination."

You can't make this crap up!

There was Harry Smith at CBS (who once did a commentary for *CBS Morning News* in which he compared the
United States to South Africa under apartheid), who
sounded like he was honored just to be in the same area
code when Obama delivered his acceptance speech for the
Democratic nomination to a packed house at Invesco Field
in Denver. "I'm just not so sure I've ever witnessed anything
like this in all of the politics that I've covered, which goes
back quite a few years," Harry gushed. "There were certain
points during the speech when the stadium was just so alive,
and the ground was almost quaking."

There was David Gergen (whom Rush Limbaugh calls
David *Rodham* Gergen) on CNN, who managed to make
Harry Smith sound (almost) like a real journalist when he
rhapsodized that Obama's Denver speech was so much more
than ... well ... a speech. "In many ways," Gergen raved, "it
was less a speech than a symphony. It moved quickly, it had
high tempo, at times inspiring, then it became more intimate, slower.... It was a masterpiece."

The tone was so syrupy you could come down with dia-
betes just sitting in your living room listening to this stuff.

But if you didn't trust your own eyes and ears, how about
what the guys in white lab coats call "scientific content

analysis"? Several non-partisan organizations looked at thousands of campaign stories that showed up in print and on the air. Take a wild guess at what they found.

The Project for Excellence in Journalism looked at more than 2,400 stories from forty-eight news outlets during a critical six-week period of the campaign—after the national political conventions in early September through the final presidential debates in mid-October. Like Captain Renault "discovering" that there's gambling going on in the back room at Rick's Café in Casablanca, I was "shocked" by their central finding: in media reporting, Barack Obama = good, and John McCain = bad.

The study concluded that while only 29 percent of the "quotations, assertions and innuendoes" in stories about Obama were negative, nearly twice as many—57 percent— of the references to McCain were negative. (Predictably, an author of that study insisted this was not because of liberal media bias. It was because Obama was leading, and "winning begets winning coverage.")

A report on the *Washington Post*'s campaign coverage by Debroah Howell, the paper's ombudsman, turned up more pro-Obama bias. "Obama deserved tougher scrutiny than he got," Howell reported in the *Post* on November 9, "especially of his undergraduate years, his start in Chicago and his relationship with Antoin 'Tony' Rezko, who was convicted this year of influence-peddling in Chicago." On the *Post*'s op-ed page, Howell counted fifty-eight clearly negative pieces about McCain, but just thirty-two negative pieces about Obama. There were also thirty-two op-ed pieces favoring Obama, but just thirteen favoring McCain.

Nice timing, I thought. The report comes out on the weekend *after* the election! What took so long? Or as Bill O'Reilly put it, "Ms. Howell and everybody else at the *Washington Post* knew the paper was trying to get Obama elected. So why didn't anybody try to stop it. Contrition *after the fact* is useless, is it not?"

Another survey, this one by the Center for Media and Public Affairs at George Mason University in Virginia, discovered on television something it called "Obama-mania." Of the 585 network news stories the Center looked at between August 23 and September 30, Obama got 65 percent favorable coverage, compared to just 36 percent positive for McCain.

Breaking it down by network, at CBS 73 percent of the comments were favorable toward Obama, versus only 31 percent toward McCain. At NBC, it was 56 percent positive for Obama, 16 percent for McCain. At ABC News, Obama got 57 percent favorable coverage, McCain 42 percent.

"For whatever reason, the media are portraying Barack Obama as a better choice for president than John McCain," concluded Robert Lichter, who conducted the Center for Media and Public Affairs study.

"For whatever reason"? How about this reason: journalists are liberal, they vote overwhelmingly for Democrats, and they like the idea of helping elect liberal Democrats who share their views, especially when the liberal Democrat could become the first black president of the United States. *That's the reason!*

McCain and his running mate, Sarah Palin, couldn't even catch a break from comedians. Another survey found that late-night comics told seven times more jokes skewering the McCain-Palin ticket than they did the Obama-Biden ticket.

And if that doesn't make you laugh, neither will this: it wasn't only the media's unbridled admiration that was masquerading as serious reporting and intelligent commentary. There also was all that inconvenient stuff a lot of the big, mainstream media didn't find all that interesting—the stories about associations and alliances between Obama and some pretty shady characters, including his anti-American, racist minister, an unrepentant domestic terrorist, and as the *Washington Post* belatedly noted, an associate charged with influence-peddling. Those were just a few of the stories that didn't interest the mainstream media all that much.

But let's be fair. We need to cut those hard-working newsmen and women some slack. They were tied up investigating really important things, like the personal financial situation of Joe the Plumber, a man who had the unmitigated gall to ask Obama the kind of tough questions that journalists would not.

The slant was too much even for liberal Democrats like the political commentator Kirsten Powers, who accused the media of "incredible bias" both for its pro-Obama coverage and also for the way it downplayed stories that might hurt the Democratic ticket—stories, for example, about how dopey Joe Biden was sounding on the campaign trail. The media wrote off these gaffes as nothing more than "Joe being Joe"—while they were jumping all over Sarah Palin for not knowing what the hell the Bush Doctrine was. (Dripping with snooty condescension, Charles Gibson of ABC News had quizzed Palin about the Bush Doctrine. However, as noted by Charles Krauthammer, who arguably invented the phrase "Bush Doctrine," Gibson himself got it wrong.)

Charlie Cook, the well-respected, longtime Washington political journalist, admitted candidly, "Let's face it, is there a Democratic and liberal bias in the media? Of course there is."

The toughest piece I saw during the whole campaign came from Michael S. Malone, a fourth generation journalist who writes for the ABC News website. "The traditional media is playing a very, very dangerous game. With its readers, with the Constitution, and with its own fate," his piece began. "The sheer bias in the print and television coverage of this election campaign is not just bewildering, but appalling. And over the last few months I've found myself slowly moving from shaking my head at the obvious one-sided reporting, to actually shouting at the screen of my television and my laptop computer."

Malone was expressing the frustrations of lots of Americans whose complaint was with bias, not with reporters asking tough questions. Was Sarah Palin qualified to be vice president? That was a legitimate question. Was John McCain too old to take on such a demanding job as president of the United States? No problem asking that one either. As far as I'm concerned, the media had an obligation to examine the hell out of the McCain-Palin ticket. Too bad they weren't nearly as vigilant with the other side.

"[N]othing, *nothing* I've seen has matched the media bias on display in the current Presidential campaign," Malone wrote. "Republicans are justifiably foaming at the mouth over the sheer one-sidedness of the press coverage of the two candidates and their running mates. But in the last few days, even Democrats, who have been gloating over the pass—no, make that shameless support—they've gotten from the press, are starting to get uncomfortable as they realize that no one wins in the long run when we don't have a free *and fair* press."

I plan to show Malone's piece to some of those guys who work the overnight shift at 7-11. There's a better chance they will understand the dire implications, for journalism and the American people, than any of those clueless wonders who run so many of America's newsrooms.

Chapter Two

PANSY BALL

I t isn't his yelling that makes Chris Matthews so goofy. It isn't the constant interruptions, either. It isn't even his coma-inducing questions that go on for a month and a half. No, what makes Chris Matthews truly a one-of-a-kind journalistic embarrassment is his total inability to understand just how embarrassing he is. He is, in a word, clueless.

Chris fancies himself a guy who knows politics and knows how to play hardball, hence the title of his show on MSNBC. "I've been following politics since I was about 5," he once bragged. And he really does know a lot about the nuts and bolts of politics, having worked for the Democrat and former House Speaker Tip O'Neill before he entered journalism. But the fact is, despite his time spent on Capitol Hill, Chris Matthews has a way of coming off as the shallowest political analyst on all of television—a medium where shallow usually is good enough to get by.

But this time, Chris Matthews made himself look even more foolish than usual.

Let's start with a remark by Matthews that has become an American classic, like the Edsel became an American classic. It happened on February 12, 2008, after Obama swept what they were calling the Potomac Primary, winning in Maryland, Virginia, and Washington, D.C., all on the same night. Matthews had just heard Obama give a victory speech and had to share his innermost thoughts—no, make that his innermost *feelings*—with all of us.

"I felt this thrill going up my leg," Matthews blurted out.

Yes, Chris heard a politician speak and it sent a thrill running up his leg. Memo to Chris Matthews: This is not political analysis. This is a man crush!

Matthews, who might as well have been wearing a short skirt and carrying pom-poms emblazoned with a big O, was madly in love with Obama and he didn't care if the whole world knew it.

This was not the first time Matthews had gushed in public over Obama. A month earlier, after Obama won the Iowa Caucus, Matthews went on the *Tonight Show* and told Jay Leno, "If you're actually in the room when [Obama] gives one of his speeches and you don't cry, you're not an American."

Got that you right-wing bastards? If you don't break down and weep when you hear the Messiah speak then you're not a *real* American. Love it or leave it, you fascist pigs!

Can you imagine if someone from FOX News had said something like that, even about the most charismatic conservative leaders? *"If you were actually in the room when Ronald Reagan gave one of his speeches and you didn't cry, you're not an American."* How the Left would howl! FOX News, they would scream, is a journalistic disgrace, a wholly owned subsidiary of the Republican National Party. But, while even his liberal colleagues giggled at Matthews' girlish swoon for Obama, the journalists in the mainstream media never acknowledged that in 2008, MSNBC, a division of NBC News, had become the unofficial television mouthpiece for the Obama campaign. But then, why should mainstream journalists make waves when they wanted Obama to win as much as anyone at MSNBC did?

Matthews also told Leno that night that Barack and Michelle Obama are, "cool people. They are really cool. They're Jack and Jackie Kennedy when you see them together. They are cool. And they're great looking and they're cool.... Everything seems to be great. I know I'm selling him now. I'm not supposed to sell."

I disagree. Hookers sell all the time. That's what they do. And Chris Matthews, whatever else he may or may not be, is a journalist hooker who was putting out for Obama from the moment the senator showed some leg and decided to run for president of the United States.

And before Matthews was done for the night, he morphed right before our eyes from Mr. Hardball into Ms. Winfrey, telling Leno, "If you're in [a room] with Obama, you feel the spirit moving."

When I'm in a room with Chris Matthews—even if it's just in my living room with Matthews babbling on TV—I feel something else moving: my lunch—moving up from my stomach, through my esophagus, and out my mouth.

And right after the election, Matthews told Joe Scarborough, "You know what? I want to do everything I can to make this presidency work." When Scarborough asked if it was Matthews' job to make Obama's presidency work, Matthews replied, "Yeah, that's my job, because this country needs a successful presidency more than anything right now."

Okay, Chris Matthews is a commentator, which gives him some leeway. Still, his slobbering prompted this dead-on reply from Howard Kurtz in his *Washington Post* media column: "Funny, it's hard to recall many journalists saying they wanted to make Ronald Reagan's or George W. Bush's presidency work."

Poor Chris. He just doesn't get it. That's why someone desperately needs to tell him that this journalistic drooling—over a *politician* no less—is not Hardball. It's Pansy Ball.

Chapter Three

GOOD NIGHT
AND GO ...

A nd then there's Keith Olbermann. When you think of MSNBC you think of Olbermann. That's how it works in cable television. "The dominant personality puts an identifying stamp on the entire organization. The stamp at MSNBC is indisputably that of Keith Olbermann." So wrote Peter Boyer in a *New Yorker* profile of Olbermann in June 2008—a piece appropriately titled, "One Angry Man."

Olbermann's critics think he is mentally ill and should be doing his show from a padded cell. His fans—*devotees* would be a better word—think he's the sanest guy in television news, maybe the only one with the guts to speak truth to

power. They see him as the reincarnation of the great, coura-
geous journalist Edward R. Murrow. Olbermann apparently
sees himself the same way. He ends his nightly broadcast
bidding his viewers, "Good night and good luck"—a rip-off
of Murrow's signature signoff.

While this alone would be considered proof in any court
of law that Olbermann is, at the very least, a legend in his
own mind, Olbermann himself has an entirely different perspective on the matter. Murrow did news and commentary,
both in the same broadcast. So do I, Olbermann reasons.
Murrow took on the powers of the day, like Joe McCarthy.
Me too, says Olbermann.

Except . . .

Edward R. Murrow never told a president to "shut the
hell up" in any of his commentaries. Olbermann gave that
"advice" to President Bush in one of his.

Murrow never posed a loaded question like the one
Olbermann posed about W.: "Pathological presidential liar,"
Keith wondered, "or an idiot in chief?"

I didn't know Ed Murrow. He stopped reporting for CBS
News long before I got there. But we all knew we were working "in the house that Murrow built." And even though I did-
n't know him personally, I knew from colleagues who did
work with him, journalists like Dan Rather, that Murrow was
not only a first-rate reporter, but was also one very classy guy.

Olbermann is something else.

Most big players in television news don't bother respond-
ing to total strangers who send hate mail. It's hard to imagine
an irate Tom Brokaw tearing into some guy because he called
Tom a jerk. Olbermann is different. When he received some
unflattering e-mails, he responded, according to the *New York*

Daily News and *Rolling Stone*, with a few e-mails of his own. He reportedly told one critic, "Go fuck your mother." To another he simply wrote, "Kill yourself." And to a third, Olbermann e-mailed, "You couldn't be stupider, wronger or dumber." (He later apologized for his intemperate messages.)

Olbermann reminds me of another angry character who used to work in television—the fictional one from the movie *Network*, who was "mad as hell" and wasn't "going to take this anymore." Keith Olberman is Howard Beale—without the charm. (For what it's worth, this is the Wikipedia reference to Beale: "During the movie, Howard struggles with depression and insanity, but his producers, rather than give him the medical help he needs, use him as a tool for getting higher ratings." Why does the phrase "life imitating art" keep popping into my head?)

I admit it. I don't get Olbermann. He's smart. He got into Cornell when he was sixteen. He's a very good writer and an innovative broadcaster who breaks through the clutter. So, why then is he so damn mean-spirited?

Actually, you don't need a *media* analyst to understand what makes Olbermann tick. You need a *psycho*analyst. It would be a scary journey, I suspect, into some very dark places. It's a trip I have no desire to take. My interest in Olbermann is entirely journalistic. It lies in the fact that he is the biggest draw on a cable news network that my friend and Olbermann's arch-enemy, Bill O'Reilly, calls, "the most biased network in the history of America."

•   •   •

But is that a fair description of MSNBC—or is it simply Bill taking a shot at the competition?

Let's start with an impartial third party. The Project for Excellence in Journalism found that MSNBC gave McCain the most negative news coverage of any television network. During the six weeks between early September and mid-October, 73 percent of all the stories on MSNBC about McCain were negative; only 14 percent of the stories about Obama were negative.

Those are astounding numbers. More than seven out of ten references to McCain were negative! It could have been worse, I guess—but not much worse. And that was for MSNBC as a whole. On Olbermann's show, it's a safe bet, the statistics would be close to 100 percent negative for McCain and 100 percent positive for Obama.

In other words, more than any other news outlet on television, MSNBC was in the tank for Obama.

What about FOX News, the network Olbermann once said was "worse than al Qaeda—worse for our society. It's as dangerous as the Ku Klux Klan ever was." Wasn't FOX News just as biased during the campaign—but in the opposite direction? As it turns out, not at all. The Project for Excellence in Journalism reported that 40 percent of FOX News's stories on McCain were negative—and 40 percent on Obama were negative.

Sure, Sean Hannity was rooting for McCain, hammering away at Obama every night for months. But Alan Colmes, the genial lefty, was rooting for Obama. As for O'Reilly, if you tuned in on any night during the campaign, you would see conservative *and* liberal commentators on the *Factor*. Not so on Olbermann's *Countdown*, where the host talks almost exclusively to liberal journalists and other people who agree with him.

Despite the overwhelming bias, there were a few bright spots at MSNBC over the course of the 2008 campaign. During the day, you got conflicting points of view from guests on various shows. And on the weekend, Alex Witt did a fair news program. Chuck Todd, MSNBC's political director, struck me as a fair-minded journalist, too. Additionally, *Morning Joe* could be smart and interesting. Sure, most of the guests were pulling for Obama, but Joe Scarborough, a former Republican congressman from Pensacola, Florida, brought a little ideological diversity to the network.

But when it came to its big money shows and campaign news coverage, MSNBC didn't even try to pretend it wasn't part of the Obama campaign.

After the first presidential debate, NBC News correspondent Andrea Mitchell told MSNBC viewers that Obama came off as "genial." Fair enough. In contrast, Chris Matthews described McCain as a "troll." And in case his insult slipped by some viewers unnoticed, Matthews repeated it—two more times.

"Do you think he was too troll-like tonight?" he asked his co-panelists on MSNBC. "You know, too much of a troll...sitting there angrily, grumpily, like a codger?...Is every press conference going to be like that, a troll-like performance, angry at the world?"

After Obama delivered his speech at Invesco Field, Olbermann intoned, "For forty-two minutes not a sour note, and spellbinding throughout in a way usually reserved for the creation of fiction." Then turning to his sidekick Chris Matthews, Olbermann said, "I'd love to find something to criticize about it. You got anything?"

Keith Olbermann would "love to find something to criticize" about Obama's speech? I don't think so. But Matthews upped the ante, taking his praise of Obama into a Biblical realm: "You know, I've been criticized for saying he [Obama] inspires me, and to hell with my critics!... You know in the Bible they talk about Jesus serving the good wine last. I think the Democrats did the same."

Yes, commentators are allowed to comment, obviously. They are entitled to their opinions. They are not bound by the same rules and standards that apply to news reporters. But even the liberal Bill Maher, who once called Sarah Palin a "stewardess" and was no fan of John McCain, was ready to puke at the unbridled adulation for Obama. "The coverage... that I was watching from MSNBC," he said, "I mean these guys were ready to have sex with him."

But perhaps the most egregious offense came when Palin was being rolled out as McCain's choice for vice president. I was watching MSNBC that day when I noticed a graphic pop up on the screen right underneath images of McCain and Palin. I couldn't believe my eyes. It said, in big bold letters: "BREAKING NEWS: HOW MANY HOUSES WILL PALIN ADD TO THE REPUBLICAN TICKET?"

This referred to a common left-wing attack on McCain, who at one point during the campaign was asked how many houses he and his wife owned and told the reporter he'd get back to him on that. But the graphic wasn't on the Jon Stewart comedy news show or on Jay Leno's *Tonight Show*. This was on MSNBC—and not during the prime time opinion shows, but during the day, during hard news political coverage, on a network supposedly devoted to *real* news.

I'm not suggesting that an executive at NBC News ordered some underling to put that graphic on the screen to embarrass McCain. I'm more than willing to believe that this was the work of one lone dummy. But even a dummy would have more brains than to do something like that unless he thought it would be deemed funny—or more important, *acceptable*—by the people who sign his paychecks.

So who's to blame for the journalistic malpractice at MSNBC? Lots of people. Jeffrey Immelt, the head of General Electric, MSNBC's parent company, could have put his foot down and insisted on a modicum of fairness from his cable news operation that, after all, is part of NBC News. But corporate executives, traditionally, don't get involved in news matters. Jeff Zucker, who produced the *Today Show* before he became head of NBC Universal, apparently didn't tell anyone to knock off the bias, either. But I understand what motivates men like Immelt and Zucker. They're businessmen. To them, news is a commodity, not unlike a GE light bulb. All they care about is whether the product makes money.

But what about Steve Capus, the president of NBC News, who is supposed to be a journalist?

"I think we're onto something," Capus told the *New Yorker*, referring to one of Olbermann's left-wing diatribes that got lots of favorable reaction from the fever swamps of the Left. "That's what we keep hearing from the audience more and more, is that they appreciate that we have people who are actually speaking truth to power or being transparent in their own personal viewpoints." Or to put it another way, MSNBC had stumbled upon a business model: make the cable network the broadcast magnet for America's angry liberals.

But surely Capus had to understand that the line between news and commentary is a bright one and that the two need to be kept separate. Olbermann's show—and the other opinion shows—as far as Capus was concerned, was like the opinion page in a newspaper. *News* was what MSNBC did the *rest of the day*. Fair enough. But if he really believed that, why did he decide to let two rabid partisans— Keith Olbermann and Chris Matthews—anchor MSNBC's hard news political coverage during the entire primary season? (FOX News, for all the faults liberals attribute to that network, never let Bill O'Reilly or Sean Hannity anchor political coverage on primary election nights.) And Capus actually planned to let Matthews and Olbermann anchor MSNBC's coverage on election night itself—until he changed his mind, with the "help" of Tom Brokaw.

As media critic Jeff Bercovici put it, "The divide between news and editorial is one of the fundamentals of journalism. Some people are able to move back and forth across that divide, taking care not to allow their personal views to color their news reportage. Olbermann (who had criticized Republicans for running 9/11 footage at their National Convention) is evidently not one of those people." Neither is Chris Matthews, Bercovi suggested. "MSNBC," he wrote, "has finally come to its senses and taken Keith Olbermann and Chris Matthews off anchor duty."

But Capus made that decision only after Brokaw made clear to him that enough was enough. Olbermann's partisan rants and Matthews' gooey commentary were one thing. But having these two yahoos anchor political coverage on the most important news night of the year, the night Americans choose a president of the United States, was a disaster waiting to happen. They were emotionally incapable of playing it straight and everybody including Tom Brokaw knew it. If their guy won, they'd be screaming and giggling like young girls at a Jonas Brothers concert. So on election night, Capus put chief White House correspondent David Gregory in the MSBNC anchor chair.

As for Olbermann, right after the election, NBC extended his contract through the next presidential election and upped his salary from $4 million a year to $7.5 million.

So was Bill O'Reilly correct? Is MSNBC "the most biased network in the history of America?" Don't look for an answer from any of the mainstream media writers, who hate O'Reilly and think MSNBC is just wonderful. It took a comedian to state the obvious. In his opening monologue right after the election, Jay Leno quipped that the Obama people were holding a victory party at their headquarters: MSNBC!

• • •

I suspect that sometime down the road Keith Olbermann is going to go too far and blow up his lucrative MSNBC career in an outburst of righteous indignation that even the money boys on executive row won't be able to tolerate. But I could be wrong. When it comes to show business, after all, nobody knows anything, as William Goldman, who wrote *Butch Cassidy and the Sundance Kid*, once said. But for now, Olbermann is the go-to guy at MSNBC. He makes money for the network, and that's all that counts.

So here's a piece of advice for Olbermann, who goes on the air each night channeling (in his mind anyway) the sainted Edward R. Murrow. Murrow once said, "Just because your voice reaches halfway around the world doesn't mean you are wiser than when it reached only to the end of the bar." Think about that, Keith, the next time you go on one of your wild and crazy harangues against conservatives. And, whatever you do, get the anger under control before you sign off. You wouldn't want to still be in a rage-induced fog when you lean into the camera the way Murrow used to and inadvertently tell your faithful fans, "Good night and go F yourselves."

Chapter Four

WHITE LIBERAL GUILT

I try not to talk politics with my liberal friends, especially the ones who work in journalism. It's not just that I find what they say annoyingly predictable, it's also that I don't like the way they look down their elite noses at "ordinary" Americans. Talking to liberals about politics for more than ten seconds brings me down. So I often announce to them in advance, "No politics!" Usually they think I'm kidding and just keep talking. But when I put my hands over my ears and start whistling "Mack the Knife," they finally figure out that I really mean it.

But sometimes you just can't avoid political conversations—which brings us to Tuesday, October 21, two weeks before Election Day. I was in New York City that day, at the HBO studios, when a liberal journalist I know spotted me and, referring to the upcoming election, asked, "So how's it going to go?"

Instead of whistling or simply walking away, which would have been the smart thing, I foolishly answered. "One of two ways," I told him. "Either Barack Obama just plain wins—or he wins big, in a blowout. I don't know which. But those are the only two possibilities."

He smiled at the good news. I smiled, too, because I thought we were done. Silly me.

He then got to the point he'd been itching to make all along. "And if he doesn't win, you know what the reason will be," he said.

"Let me guess—racism!"

He smiled again. What else could it be?

This is why I choose not to talk to liberals about anything important unless I have to. I politely told my journalist friend—a smart and very nice guy—that "yes, in a country of more than 300 million people we're going to have some racists. But not that many. Not anymore. And having a few yahoos here or there certainly doesn't make this a racist country."

He didn't buy any of it—he was worried that hordes of bigots just might crawl out from under their rocks and steal a great historic moment away from all of us. I guess it didn't register with him, or with the other liberals who think this is a fundamentally racist country, that America— a nation that is still predominantly white, a nation where blacks make up only about 12 percent of the population—

was (according to the polls) on the verge of electing a black man as president of the United States. And not just any black man, but one whose name was Barack Hussein Obama.

How racist can a country be that is willing to do that?

This doesn't mean I'm unaware of our racial history. It doesn't mean I don't understand how nasty it was, or that I don't grasp the significance of America's original sin—slavery—or the injustice that was segregation. Like most of us, I get all that. But I also understand how far we've come in this country. I understand that lots of liberals voted for Obama over Hillary Clinton, who pretty much had the same liberal views, *precisely because he is black*. They wanted to make a statement with their vote. But while liberals like to call themselves progressives, when it comes to race they are stuck in the past.

Millions of us did not vote for Obama for just one reason—we didn't like his liberal politics. Race had nothing to do with our decision. Nothing! Yet liberal reporters and pundits—the very people who keep telling us we need to get beyond race in this country—seemed incapable of doing it.

Just before the Democratic National Convention in August 2008, Jacob Weisberg wrote a piece for *Slate* entitled, "If Obama Loses." Right under that headline was this subtitle: "Racism is the only reason McCain might beat him." So if McCain had won, what would the message have been to both America and the outside world that was watching? That a Republican beat a Democrat? That a (sort of) conservative beat a liberal? That more Americans liked McCain's policies than Obama's? No, no, and no. The message would have been that Obama lost because racism continues to hang over our country like a poisonous cloud.

●   ●   ●

A few bigots yell something nasty at a McCain or Palin rally and it was national news—the *New York Times* pronounced the Republican candidates guilty of "race baiting."

But that wasn't all. In 2008, almost any Republican criticism of Obama or his associates was met with outraged accusations of racism from the mainstream media. If the Republicans talked about the bomber Bill Ayers, they were race baiting. If they talked about the illegal voter registration drives of ACORN, they were race baiting. If their surrogates brought up the Reverend Wright, they were race baiting. If they had cast doubt on global warming they probably would have been accused of race baiting, too.

The liberal media imposed a blatant double standard on Republicans. McCain and Palin were responsible for what came out of the mouths of people at their rallies, even though they were total strangers to them. But as Charles Krauthammer noted, "Should you bring up Barack Obama's real associations—20 years with Jeremiah Wright, working on two foundations and distributing money with William Ayers, citing the raving [Father] Michael Pfleger as one who helps him keep his moral compass (*Chicago Sun Times*, April 2004) and the long-standing relationship with left-wing vote-fraud specialist ACORN—you have crossed the line into illegitimate guilt by association. Moreover, it is tinged with racism."

And when McCain ran a light-hearted campaign ad that portrayed Obama as a mere celebrity—and used a picture of Paris Hilton and Britney Spears to drive home the point—*New York Times* columnist Bob Herbert saw nasty, old-fashioned racism. It was an attempt, Herbert wrote, "to exploit the hostility, anxiety and resentment of the many white Americans who are still freakishly hung up on the idea of black men rising above their station and becoming sexually involved with white women."

Huh?

I interviewed Herbert once when I was working at CBS News. He's a very nice, smart, civil guy. But this is *nuts*! Everybody—including the *astute* folks at the *New York Times*—knows that McCain could very easily have gone after the Reverend Wright, a black man who said the U.S. government created AIDS in order to kill off black people and that "America's chickens were coming home to roost" when we were attacked on 9/11. But McCain refused to do it, probably to his own detriment. As Krauthammer put it, "McCain has denied himself the use of that perfectly legitimate issue. It is simply Orwellian for him to be now so widely vilified as a stoker of racism."

No good deed, I guess, goes unpunished.

When Palin poked fun at "community organizers" in her acceptance speech for the Republican nomination for vice president, she was accused of veiled racism. Chris Matthews wondered if this was Republican code, were community organizers "the new welfare queen," he demanded to know.

My God, these liberals are not only paranoid, they are in desperate need of a sense of humor transplant. They see racism everywhere!

There were even suggestions, including one by Bob Herbert's colleague on the *Times*'s op-ed page, Paul Krugman, that when Joe the Plumber said he thought Obama had "tap danced almost as good as Sammy Davis Jr." in trying to explain what he meant by "spreading the wealth," that this too was racist. Get it? Liberals think only black people tap dance. Sammy Davis is black. Hence, Joe the Plumber is a racist and by extension so is McCain, because Joe the Plumber was his ally.

Someone get a judge to sign the commitment papers against these liberal whack-jobs (and maybe assign them to watch some old Gene Kelly and Fred Astaire movies, too).

And when Obama preemptively asserted that Republicans would use his race against him, that they would say, "He's young and inexperienced and he's got a funny name. And did I mention, he's black?"—something neither McCain nor Palin ever said—the Obama media continued to tell us that he alone was America's hope, that he was the "post-racial candidate" who, if he should loose, would be the victim of American racism.

George Orwell must be spinning in his grave.

There are deep reasons why so many white journalists sold out their principles for Obama. In no small way, they were trying to redeem their own racial virtue. "Since the sixties, whites have had to prove a negative—that they are *not* racist," is how the scholar Shelby Steele explained it in an essay entitled, "Liberal Bias and the Zone of Decency."

According to Steele, white liberals desperately try to show "good racial manners," which is part of something he calls "deferential liberalism." This is how white people, and in this case white slobbering journalists, show how decent they themselves are. "That peculiar, post-sixties deferential liberalism," Steele writes, "has been more interested in redeeming the moral authority of whites than in actually helping blacks."

Sure, they wanted to make their Messiah look good. But even more important, they wanted to *feel* good—*about themselves*!

Funny, though, I don't remember the media fretting about good racial manners or exhibiting deferential liberalism when Michael Steele, a black man, lost his race for the Senate in Maryland in 2006. I don't recall any journalists bemoaning that a historical moment was lost when Lynn Swann, another black man, lost his race for governor of Pennsylvania, also in 2006. Or when Kenneth Blackwell, who is also black, lost his race for governor of Ohio that same year. I don't recollect any angst at all that these three *conservative* black men went down to defeat, even though they all lost to plain old white guys.

Where were the cries from liberal journalists about history being thwarted? Where was the outrage that voters in Maryland, Pennsylvania, and Ohio had rejected three decent black men?

But liberals don't really see conservative black men as black—anymore than they see conservative women as women. They see them as only as *conservatives*. So they don't really count.

That's why journalists could be moved by Obama's election in a way they could never be moved when a black man named Clarence Thomas made it from poverty all the way to the Supreme Court of the United States. That's why Condoleezza Rice isn't a media hero. Trust me, if Condi were a liberal Democrat, she would be on the cover of *Time* every other week, which was about as often as the magazine put Obama on its cover during the 2008 campaign.

Imagine, just for a moment, that the conservative African-American Michael Steele had become the first black president of these United States of America instead of Obama. Do you think we would have heard nearly as much about it being a great historical moment? Do you think Mike Barnicle would be telling us about what "a great reflection [this is] of us as a country"?

I don't.

If liberal journalists were honest, they would admit that they see black conservatives as racial sellouts. But Obama, the most liberal member of the U.S. Senate—more liberal than Bernie Sanders, the socialist from Vermont—is just the kind of black man they could get behind and support for president.

And that's exactly what they did.

Chapter Five

PDS

Part way through the campaign, just after Sarah Palin was picked as McCain's choice for vice president, a strange mental disorder spread through many parts of liberal America, including the nation's newsrooms.

The disorder came to be known simply as PDS, short for Palin Derangement Syndrome. PDS was similar to BDS, Bush Derangement Syndrome, a mental illness that struck millions of liberals, mainly in places like Manhattan and Hollywood, and left them foaming at the mouth at the mere mention of the president's name. Palin Derangement Syndrome was just like that.

Liberal politicians, as you might imagine, suffered from serious bouts of PDS.

Lincoln Chafee, the liberal Republican senator from Rhode Island who quit the party after losing re-election in 2006 and became an Obama supporter, muttered something about Palin being a "cocky whacko."

The chairwoman of the South Carolina Democratic Party, Carol Fowler, maliciously declared that Palin's "primary qualification seems to be that she hasn't had an abortion."

And when Charlie Rangel, the liberal congressman from Harlem, was asked why Democrats were afraid of Palin and her popularity, he casually responded, "You got to be kind to the disabled."

Soon we learned that a man of God, a Catholic priest and author, had come down with full-blown PDS. Father Andrew Greeley, a left-wing clergyman in Chicago, sputtered that Palin was "a racist with her eye on the White House."

PDS even struck several highly respected political scientists in the entertainment industry.

Bill Maher barked that Palin was a "snarling bitch" who needed to be kept "out of the White House."

Even the usually brilliant Pamela Anderson could not escape the clutches of PDS. Exhibiting her trademark class and articulateness, Pammy said that Sarah Palin, simply, "can suck it."

The terrible disorder also struck ordinary liberals at Obama rallies. Some held up signs that read, "Abort Sarah Palin." Some wore T-shirts that proclaimed, "Sarah Palin is a . . ."—the next word being a vulgar reference to a certain part of a woman's body.

Interestingly, the mainstream media didn't seem the least bit troubled by the raving lunacy of the Left brought on by PDS. Interesting, I say, because these were the very same sensitive journalistic souls that worried about McCain and Palin stirring up "Weimar-like rage" and causing a "violent escalation of rhetoric," as Frank Rich warned in the *New York Times*; or that they just might be ushering in the "re-emergence of the far right as a power in American politics," as E. J. Dionne fretted in the *Washington Post*; or that they were appealing to crowds "gripped by insane rage," as Nobel Prize winner Paul Krugman put it in the *New York Times*.

Yes, the mental disorder had hit the mainstream media, too—as hard as that is to believe.

Maureen Dowd wrote in the *New York Times* that Palin was "our new Napoleon in bunny boots."

Us Weekly ran a cover story on Palin titled, "Baby, Lies & Scandal"—two months after the magazine ran a glowing cover story on the Obama family.

Wendy Doniger, a professor at the University of Chicago, wrote on the *Washington Post*'s website that Palin's "greatest hypocrisy is in her pretense that she is a woman."

Juan Cole, a professor at the University of Michigan, wrote a piece for *Salon*, the online magazine. "What is the difference between Palin and a Muslim fundamentalist?" he asked. "Lipstick."

Also on *Salon*, writer Cintra Wilson managed to type these words as Palin Derangement Syndrome ate away at her brain: "[Sarah Palin is] such a power-mad, backwater beauty-pageant casualty, it's easy to write her off and make fun of her. But in reality I feel as horrified as a ghetto Jew watching the rise of National Socialism."

Help me out here: that would make the rise of Sarah Palin akin to the rise of Adolf Hitler, right? Funny, I never thought of it that way. But then, *I'm not NUTS!*

And then there's Andrew Sullivan, a normally sane journalist who came down with Palin Derangement Syndrome and completely lost his marbles. On the *Atlantic* magazine website, he wrote over a dozen pieces questioning whether Trig was really Palin's baby. He called Palin a "compulsive, repetitive, demonstrable liar." And he freely admitted that she drove him around the bend. "As you can see, I've been manically blogging for months now and dealing with the Palin terror as best I can," he moaned. "She haunts my dreams, sends my stomach sinking at odd moments, terrifies me in the morning, cracks me up in the afternoon, but, if it weren't for Ambien, wonderful Ambien, would keep me awake at night."

Somebody call Jerry Lewis! We need a telethon to raise money to fight this terrible disease.

And since craziness does not respect geographical borders, PDS also turned up in Canada. Heather Mallick, a college professor, summed up the feelings of millions of American liberals in one elegant sentence, which was part of a piece she wrote on the Canadian Broadcasting Company's website. Palin, said Ms. Mallick, "added nothing to the ticket that the Republicans didn't already have sewn up, the white trash vote."

. . .

So, what was it about Sarah Palin that drove so many liberals into the throes of mental illness?

I have a theory. What drives some of them nuts is not just that they think she's unqualified to be vice president, or certainly president, of the United States. As I said before, that's a perfectly legitimate point of view.

What makes these liberals foam at the mouth is that this "white trash," pro-gun, pro-life, church-going woman, who didn't to go to Harvard or Yale or Princeton, but who flitted from one second-rate school to another before she wound up (my God, they groaned) *at the University of Idaho*, became the most prominent woman in all of America!

They hated that. It wasn't supposed to be that way. It drove them crazy with rage. She wasn't one of them. She wasn't even really a woman, as those feminists told us. She was . . . a *conservative*!

And besides, what kind of real woman has five kids? And who names her kids Track, Bristol, Willow, Piper, and Trig? The elites gasped, *"What the hell kind of low-rent names are those?"* I'll bet you can't find one kid in the entire Upper West Side of Manhattan whose name is Track, Bristol, Willow, Piper, or Trig. Not one!

And while we're on the subject, what woman in her right mind has a baby with Down Syndrome? And what kind of mother lets her unmarried teenage daughter go through with a pregnancy and have a baby? *Haven't those hicks ever heard of abortions?* Sure, well-off Manhattan kids with liberal parents get pregnant, too. But, my God, they don't actually have the baby. If you're going to Harvard (or Yale or

Princeton) in the fall, *you don't have the baby*! Everyone knows that!

And, as Dennis Miller, my fellow bloviator on FOX News, says, liberal feminists hated her because she wasn't neurotic and seemed to be happily married—*unlike most of them!*

So in the end, this wasn't about Palin at all. This was about liberals, whether they're journalists or just plain civilians. Liberals fancy themselves the good ones, the tolerant ones, the open-minded ones. But they don't really understand (or have much use for) the Sarah Palins of this country. Liberals don't really like church-going Middle Americans. Their old-fashioned decency rubs a lot of lefties the wrong way. They seem hopelessly square to those hip liberals. And they don't understand, either, why anyone would eat at Red Lobster, which to liberals is akin to a crime against humanity. They look askance at *hayseeds* in the heartland who proudly fly the flag on the Fourth of July. They snicker at ordinary folks who like to bowl.

Palin lost. Liberals can breath easy. They no longer have to suffer the torment of Palin Derangement Syndrome. But they do need to understand that the real reason they hated Palin so much was not just because of her conservative politics. More than that, they hated her because she was so much like "ordinary" Americans. And if there's one thing those good, tolerant, open-minded liberals can't stand, it's ordinary Americans.

That, at the end of the day, is their real pathology.

Chapter Six

MY CONVERSATION WITH RUSH LIMBAUGH

As part of my research for this book, I interviewed Rush Limbaugh to get his take on how the media covered—or more accurately, how they cheered on—Barack Obama. Rush is a commentator and entertainer, and he's also as astute as anyone I know on politics and the media.

I started by asking him if the media were even more biased, or biased in a different way, during the presidential election of 2008.

Limbaugh: It was worse than ever before because of the historical significance the media placed on Obama's election.

Most of the elders in the Drive Bys [Rush's term for the mainstream media] came of age during the civil rights battles of the '60s and they have taught the younger journalists to think in the same way. This is why the specifics of who Obama is, are irrelevant to them. The Drive Bys determined that this election was about *them* as much as Obama. They were also out to prove that they could still move public opinion and effect a national outcome in their favor to prove the New Media is of no consequence. And it helped immensely that Obama had no real opposition in McCain. The New Media was not motivated in support of McCain— but rather in opposition to Obama. So for us, it was a lose-lose proposition.

Goldberg: Do you think the so-called mainstream media care what the American people think of them? Do you think they give a damn that a majority of Republicans *and* Democrats think they were in the tank for Obama?

Limbaugh: Why should they give a damn? As far as the Drive Bys are concerned, this was a *huge* triumph. Their glory days are back, they think. They just succeeded in dumbing down 52 percent of the electorate to get what they wanted. They now feel more empowered than ever.

Goldberg: By anointing him, by deifying him, did they— unintentionally, of course—set him up for a fall when something goes wrong? Or will they continue to cover for him?

Limbaugh: Obama is *too big to fail.* The Drive Bys will simply not allow it. Any Obama failures will be eagerly blamed on the Bush Administration. Obama and the media will simply say, "The problems in the economy are much worse than we knew. The Bush administration was not forthcoming during the transition about all we would face." Obama will say, "We cannot close Gitmo and get out of Iraq as soon as I would have liked. I discovered many things the Bush Administration hid from public view that make immediate action impossible."

Goldberg: I would argue that the mainstream media didn't lose the election for McCain—McCain lost it for McCain, and so did Republicans who sold out their conservative principles when they took over both houses of Congress *and* the White House in 2000. So if the media didn't throw the election, why should we care what they said and wrote during the campaign?

Limbaugh: I totally agree. Had there been a genuine conservative alternative on the ballot, Obama and the media would have flamed dramatically. Candidates lose or win elections, not the media. However, the McCain campaign failed utterly in defining Obama while the media was covering for him. The historical nature of the campaign again reared its head. The McCain camp was deathly afraid of *any* criticism that could be labeled racist.

But regarding the other part of your question, Bernie: we should care what the media said and wrote during the campaign because we must *finally* [Rush sighs at this point] learn from it. And what we need to learn is that we can *never* expect a fair shot from the media, and to hope for that is just plain stupid. Republicans and conservatives must finally realize they will have *two* opponents in every election: the Democratic candidate *and* the media.

Goldberg: During the campaign, did you read or hear anything that made you think: my God, the media is even worse than I thought?

Limbaugh: Yes, so many times I cannot recount them here. But here's one example: here they were, all concerned about domestic spying against terrorists, yet they sat idly by while Ohio Democrats used the power of government to investigate and destroy a lowly *private citizen* who simply asked a question of Obama. They then piled on in the effort to destroy Joe the Plumber.

Goldberg: Any thoughts about MSNBC?

Limbaugh: I think they damaged the NBC brand but I don't think anyone over there cares about that right now, owing to their euphoria at pushing Obama over the top. MSNBC is the official network of left-wing lunatics and there are enough of them apparently to accrue enough of an audience for MSNBC to be satisfied. Their big challenge now will be to satisfy that lunatic audience without George Bush around to bitch about every night. I suspect MSNBC will now focus on the critics of Obama to continue offering meat to their deranged audience.

Goldberg: What did you make of Palin Derangement Syndrome? Why such hatred, especially from liberal feminists? Was it simply her politics or was something else at play?

Limbaugh: Something else. She was the only effective Republican anywhere in this entire campaign—among all candidates, for all offices. Sarah Palin is what militant feminists have been suggesting all women can become. But she had the gall to have a Down Syndrome child and be opposed to abortion, which is the sacrament to feminist liberalism. She was the Clarence Thomas of the Anita Hill hearings. Her electoral future had to be destroyed.

Goldberg: Is there anything—*anything*—the mainstream media can do that will help them regain the trust of the American people—and if so, will they do it?

Limbaugh: *They don't care about the trust of the American people.* The mainstream media's audience is the mainstream media. They, like all liberals, have contempt for the American people who, in their eyes, are not sophisticated enough to understand the work and importance of the mainstream media. The mainstream media exist to succeed *despite* the American people.

Bernie, I honestly believe the following: I believe that I, Rush Limbaugh, am responsible for the mainstream media's behavior today because they think I am the one who destroyed their monopoly beginning in 1988 when I started my show. Back then, we had the three nets, CNN, and the big papers. They owned what was news and what was not news. They owned commentary. Now they don't. I believe the creation of the New Media has made the mainstream media now openly competitive with the New Media, which is why they are so open now about choosing sides.

This is not my ego speaking, Bernie, but since I started in 1988, look at what has happened. There were 125 talk stations in 1988. Now there are over 2,000. Right-wing blogs have sprung up. FOX News prime time is simply talk radio on TV. So all this New Media pisses off the mainstream media. They are in open competition with us and as such have now been forced to openly declare what they used to hide behind their so-called objectivity: and that is their liberalism.

Goldberg: How long will the honeymoon between Obama and the mainstream media last?

Limbaugh: Forever! *He is too big to fail.*

Chapter Seven

HEY, I'M JUST ASKING...

Do you think the media would have paid more attention if it were the National Rifle Association, instead of ACORN, that signed Mickey Mouse up to vote?

Do you think the mainstream media would have shown more interest if it were John McCain, and not Barack Obama, who had a relationship, no matter how flimsy, with an unrepentant terrorist?

Would the media think it was old news if this terrorist had helped kick off *McCain's* political career?

What if the terrorist had bombed not the Capitol and Pentagon but a *black church or an abortion clinic*—no matter how long ago it was?

And what would the media say if on September 11, 2001, of all days, a story came out in the *New York Times* in which this bomber said his only regret from those days was that he didn't do more?

What would the media say about all that?

How would the media play the story had it been *John McCain* who spent twenty years in a church with a *right-wing* minister who said racist things about *black* people?

What if it were *Sarah Palin*, and not Joe Biden, who stood before a cheering crowd of *conservatives* and said the solution to our economic woes could be summed up in "a three-letter word: jobs"—and then went on to spell the word out loud: "J-O-B-S."

Or what if it were *Sarah Palin*, and not Joe Biden, who said that in 1929 Franklin Roosevelt "got on the television" to reassure the American people "when the stock market crashed"—even though FDR didn't take office until 1933 and television wasn't introduced to the general public until 1939?

How would the mainstream media treat that story? You think they might portray her as a moron? Or worse, a ticking time bomb?

The questions, of course, require no answers. Because we all know that the same mainstream media that slavishly tried to make the Democratic ticket look good would have been all over each of these stories—since they all would have made Republicans look bad.

But what many of us call bias, journalists simply call *news judgment*. They weren't shilling or covering for Obama, they say. They were merely making *editorial decisions*. And they decided that Wright, and Ayers, and ACORN, and Biden's gaffes were not worthy of a lot of coverage.

Take the Reverend Wright story. On May 5, 2008, John Roberts on CNN summed up the feelings of a lot of mainstream journalists when he told Obama, "I want to just stipulate at the beginning of this interview we are declaring a Reverend Wright free zone today. So, no questions about Reverend Wright. . . . Is that okay with you?

Obama obligingly responded, "Fair enough. That sounds just fine."

Or how about the Bill Ayers story?

On October 31, 2008, just four days before the election, I tried an experiment. I ran a check to see how many stories the *New York Times*—the newspaper of record—had recently run on Ayers, and how many the paper ran on Palin's wardrobe, which some commentators argued was a waste of a lot of money for the McCain campaign.

It turns out that during the previous ten days, the *Times* ran eleven news stories on Palin's wardrobe and three additional op-ed columns. But in the previous *two months*, those impartial folks at the *Times* ran only two stories examining the relationship between Ayers and Obama. Perhaps two was enough—but *eleven* news stories on Palin's clothing? Why did they think that story was worth so much more ink?

The fact is, there is a whole array of stories that conservatives find important but liberals in the mainstream media don't. Needless to say, editors have every right to decide what they think real news is. Just because some people want stories about Paris Hilton or Britney Spears doesn't mean the editors of the *New York Times* or the *Washington Post* should run mindless celebrity gossip about those two. But Wright and Ayers aren't Hilton and Spears, are they?

Thomas Sowell, the scholar based at the Hoover Institution in Palo Alto, California, noted that "although Senator Barack Obama has been allied with a succession of far left individuals over the years, that is only half the story. There are, after all, some honest and decent people on the left. But these have not been the ones that Obama has been allied with—allied, not merely 'associated' with."

ACORN, Sowell noted, is not just a grassroots organization that registers Americans to vote: "In addition to the voter frauds that ACORN has been involved in over the years, it is an organization with a history of thuggery, including going to bankers' homes to harass them and their families, in order to force banks to lend to people with low credit ratings."

In light of the key role such lending practices played in the current economic meltdown, one would think the media would find ACORN newsworthy. But one would be wrong. Just as one would be wrong to think the media was much interested in the keen support Fannie Mae and Freddie Mac received from Obama, who was the second biggest recipient of lobbying money from those two key players in the housing bust that has damaged the entire economy.

Then there are Obama's spiritual mentors. "Jeremiah Wright and [Father] Michael Pfleger are not just people with left-wing opinions," Sowell pointed out. "They are reckless demagogues preaching hatred of the lowest sort—and both are recipients of money from Obama."(This referred to the foundation, the Chicago Annenberg Challenge, that Obama helped run with his friend Bill Ayers.)

And "Bill Ayers is not just 'an education professor' who has some left-wing views," according to Sowell. "He is a confessed and unrepentant terrorist, who more recently has put his message of resentment into the schools—an effort, using money from a foundation that Obama headed."

This should have been the stuff of serious, probing stories in the mainstream media. Instead, if they reported on these alliances at all, it was with great reluctance. But how can a big newspaper or a major network news division write off such a large chunk of the American people who think these stories are important?

How can the mainstream media ignore the kinds of things a smart, conservative columnist like Thomas Sowell wrote about and still be taken seriously by the millions of other conservatives who constitute an important segment of the American mainstream?

The answer is simple. They can't.

Chapter Eight

JEREMIAH WRIGHT AND THE MEDIA

DON'T TELL, DON'T ASK

Thanks to the New Media, by now everyone knows about the Reverend Jeremiah Wright and his anti-American rants. Sure, if he sounded like Harry Reid nobody would care what he had to say. But unlike Harry, Wright is a man of enormous charisma with the ability to work up a crowd, a gift especially dangerous when possessed by a demagogue. Here is a man who could stand in the pulpit on a Sunday morning and read a grocery list, and the power of his voice alone would make his congregants want to run out to the nearest supermarket and buy peanut butter, jelly, cookies, soup, and everything else on the damn list.

And if Wright had simply been a pastor in Chicago, per-haps his theories about how we brought 9/11 on ourselves and about how our government created AIDS to eradicate black people would have been of little concern. After all, we probably wouldn't have even known about this oddball preacher in the first place. And if somehow we had heard of him, we probably would have written him off as just one more paranoid screwball, like the loons who thought the astronauts never landed on the moon, that it was all shot in a movie studio; or the nut-jobs who believe that the attacks on September 11, 2001, were "an inside job."

But during the 2008 presidential campaign, Wright wasn't just any preacher. He was the longtime pastor of a leading candidate to become president of the United States; a man who admired Wright and called him his mentor; a man who asked the Reverend to officiate at his wedding ceremony and baptize his children.

This is why, in early March 2008, when the whole world had finally heard about Jeremiah Wright—thanks to those videotapes that showed the minister standing in the pulpit and railing about the sins of white America—Barack Obama faced a crisis unprecedented in recent American political history.

He could not simply deny that his friend and mentor had some truly nutty ideas, or contend that Wright never really said the things he really said. The tapes were there for every-one to see and hear. It would be like Bill Clinton telling America, "I did not have sexual relations with that woman, Miss Lewinsky," after posting a videotape of their tryst on the Internet. (Thank God there was no tape!)

This was the story that would have destroyed Obama's campaign before it even began and made Hillary Clinton the Democratic Party's nominee for president. And even if Obama didn't agree with Wright's crazier statements—and he said he did not—still, there were important, legitimate questions that demanded answers from Obama: like why did he remain in Wright's church for nearly twenty years? This was a story that seemed to undermine the very premise of the Obama campaign—the notion that he was a moderate, "post-racial" candidate.

So how did Obama survive when Wright could have brought him down? Timing had a lot to do with it. By the time the tapes came out, Obama had already racked up enough victories that, mathematically, he was well on the way to securing the nomination, though the tapes certainly had hurt him, at least temporarily. In fact, after the video-tapes started running on TV, he suffered so many primary losses that Hillary came within a breath of snatching the nomination away from him.

But it wasn't just timing. The ever-friendly Obama media also played a crucial role in helping him survive—both before the tapes came out and after; before, mainly by sani-tizing Wright's radicalism; after, by very quickly declaring that Obama had dealt with all the crucial issues. The media insisted that Obama was not about *exploiting* racial division but instead was the one who could *bring us all together*—and therefore there was no more to say.

And exactly how did the media sanitize Wright when his radicalism first surfaced?

By focusing instead on non-controversial issues, like how much fun it was to go to his church.

A story in the *St. Petersburg* (Florida) *Times*, for example, quoted a parishioner as saying the church combines gospel singing and modern dance with Southern-style hand-shaking, hugging, and kissing; and that the preaching tends to be "common-sense folk wisdom laced with theological sophistication.... There's singing and shouting and people get happy," according to the parishioner interviewed by an accommodating reporter.

I'm sure it's all true, at least when the congregation wasn't getting happy over Reverend Wright maniacally shouting, "God damn America."

Most of us saw what the press was up to, even if the reporters themselves were in a state of self-denial about their own bias.

Here's what I mean: ask any reporter if he or she intentionally downplayed stories that might have made Wright look bad. After they finish rolling their eyes they'll tell you (in a way that makes clear they think you're a pathetic idiot) that they are in the business of *disseminating* information, not *hiding* it. But what they would not tell you—because most of them don't understand it—is that they work in liberal newsrooms imbued with liberal sensibilities. And so they are like fish in the ocean that don't know they're wet. How would fish know they're wet? Fish have no frame of reference. *They only know wet.*

And, yes, it is the same with the journalistic fish who swim in America's big mainstream liberal newsrooms. They don't fully understand how their liberalism affects their news judgment. And so they don't grasp a salient fact: *that as liberals they have a very difficult time dealing with black bigotry.* Consciously or otherwise, they tend to shy away from those kinds of news stories.

So when they did get around to reporting on Wright, they simply did not tell the full truth. Sure, they described him as "controversial" or "passionate" or even "fiery." But when they hinted at what made him so "controversial," they typically diverted the heaviest accusations against him—that he was a racist demagogue—onto the conservatives who dared to discuss Wright's incendiary sermons.

One especially nasty example of this approach appeared in the *Boston Globe* on January 28, 2008, in a piece by Alex Beam, who wrote that "Wright has been profiled by several newspapers, and the forward shock troops of the right-wing hate machine, i.e. FOX News, have already lobbed a few shells in his direction."

Get it, you dense right-wing dummies? Pay attention, morons! Wright was the victim! So what if he didn't seem to give a damn that his own country was attacked on September 11, 2001? So what if he believed the United States government was on a mission to commit genocide against black people? Wright wasn't the hater. The haters were those right-wingers who drew attention to his rantings, led by the mean-spirited bastards at FOX News.

Oh yeah, Mr. Beam also wrote in that same *Boston Globe* column that "for obvious reasons, Obama has had to put some distance between himself and his pastor. But to his

credit, he has not severed his ties with Wright, and there is
no indication that he will."

Really?

• • •

The first big national story about Jeremiah Wright and his
radical ideas didn't come from the *New York Times* or any
other major American newspaper. It came from *Rolling
Stone*, a publication devoted more to music than to politics.
In a thoughtful profile of Obama that appeared in the Feb-
ruary 22, 2007, issue—timed roughly to coincide with
Obama's announcement that he was running for president—
Rolling Stone reported on some of the inflammatory state-
ments Wright had been making from the pulpit of his
Chicago church:

> And there is the Rev. Jeremiah Wright, a sprawl-
> ing, profane bear of a preacher, a kind of black
> ministerial institution, with his own radio shows
> and guest preaching gigs across the country.
> Wright takes the pulpit here one Sunday and
> solemnly, sonorously declares that he will recite
> ten essential facts about the United States. "Fact
> number one: we've got more black men in prison
> than there are in college," he intones. "Fact num-
> ber two: racism is how this country was founded
> and how this country is still run!" There is
> thumping applause; Wright has a cadence and
> power that make Obama sound like John Kerry.
> Now the Reverend begins to preach. "We are

deeply involved in the importing of drugs, the exporting of guns and the training of professional KILLERS.... We believe in white supremacy and black inferiority and believe it more than we believe in God.... We conducted radiation experiments on our own people.... We care nothing about human life if the ends justify the means!" The crowd whoops and amens as Wright builds to his climax: "And. And. And! GAWD! Has got! To be SICK! OF THIS SHIT!"

So, the Reverend Wright tells his congregation that America believes in white supremacy; that it believes in black inferiority even more than it believes in God; that the United States government imports drugs; that we Americans care nothing about human life. And while he's ranting, "there is thumping applause" from a congregation that clearly loves his every word.

Okay. Now try to imagine the impact those words would have had if they appeared *not in a music magazine*, but in the most influential newspaper in the country, the *New York Times*, the newspaper that producers at ABC, NBC, and CBS News read first thing in the morning so they'll know what to cover that day. Trust me, if the *Times* went on strike one morning, they wouldn't know what to put on the *CBS Evening News* that night. Such is the influence the *Times* has on other media, especially network television news.

The *Rolling Stone* piece, entitled "The Radical Roots of Barack Obama," was smart and perceptive. "This is as openly radical a background as any significant American political figure has ever emerged from," the magazine reported, "as much Malcolm X as Martin Luther King Jr. Wright is not an incidental figure in Obama's life, or his politics. The senator 'affirmed' his Christian faith in this church; he uses Wright as a 'sounding board' to 'make sure I'm not losing myself in the hype and hoopla.' Both the title of Obama's second book, *The Audacity of Hope*, and the theme for his keynote address at the Democratic National Convention in 2004 come from Wright's sermons. 'If you want to understand where Barack gets his feeling and rhetoric from,' says the Rev. Jim Wallis, a leader of the religious left, 'just look at Jeremiah Wright.'"

That night, after the *Rolling Stone* article hit the newsstands, Katie, Brian, and Charlie should have run lead stories on Obama's longtime friend, the raving minister Jeremiah Wright. The next morning, every major newspaper in the United States should have jumped on it too, and run page one stories under headlines that announced, "Obama Tied to Anti-White, Anti-American Minister." And right next to those page one stories, they should have run long profiles of the "passionate" Reverend Wright, a man who was such an important influence on Obama.

And the only digging reporters would have had to do—to find out all the racist, anti-American things Wright was preaching—was into their wallets, to come up with a few bucks to buy the DVDs of his sermons that were on sale— *right there in the church*!

You didn't have to be Woodward or Bernstein to figure this one out.

The mainstream media's willful blindness toward Wright did not go unnoticed. A *New York Post* editorial observed that "Wright's self-professed Afrocentric church has attracted surprisingly little media attention—given the critical role that Obama says Wright and the congregation have played in his personal development. It's especially disquieting that Obama seems to be getting a free pass, even as GOP candidates like Mitt Romney and Mike Huckabee face repeated questions about their religious beliefs and associations."

The paper concluded, "Certainly, Wright's words and work should be considered fair game."

And you can be sure of one thing: if John McCain had a *right-wing* Reverend Wright in *his* life, a minister he had known for nearly twenty years and who was his spiritual guidance counselor, you can bet *that* story would have been written up large on page one of every big city newspaper in the country.

Journalists fancy themselves smarter than the average guy or gal. A lot smarter. Take my word for it, I worked with these elitists for twenty-eight years at CBS. But they didn't seem to grasp why the Wright-Obama story mattered. In their view, it would be ludicrous to believe that Obama shares Wright's views, and therefore there's no story. But the Wright-Obama story was extremely important because Obama was a political unknown—and Wright represented one of the very few clues that might tell us who this stranger really was. Even if Obama does not subscribe to Wright's overall view of America as an oppressor nation, Wright was one of his key mentors, and it's worth investigating what ideas Wright passed on to his acolyte.

Just a few years earlier virtually no one outside of Chicago politics knew anything about Obama. Now he was seeking the Democratic Party's nomination for president of the United States—and the Reverend Wright was one of the few people we knew who had influenced him. For that reason alone, the mainstream media should have shown a lot more interest than they did in Jeremiah Wright.

And, as *Rolling Stone* pointed out, Wright's influence on Obama was right there in plain view for anyone to see. All you had to do was to read Obama's book. "When you read his [Obama's] autobiography," *Rolling Stone* noted, "the surprising thing—for such a measured politician—is the depth of radical feeling that seeps through, the amount of Jeremiah Wright that's packed in there."

•   •   •

Because the story appeared in a music magazine, it attracted little attention in the mainstream media. But it did catch the attention of Obama and his handlers, a savvy group of political strategists who didn't miss anything and could sense trouble a mile away. And since this was the very same Reverend Wright who was scheduled to give the public invocation for Obama's official declaration of his candidacy on February 10, 2007, something had to be done about this potential problem.

And something was done: Obama called Wright and told him he was no longer invited to give the invocation. Wright's presence at the ceremony, Obama said, might cause problems. So Obama threw his good friend Mr. Wright under the proverbial bus.

The first time Obama's connection with Wright appeared in the *New York Times* was on March 6, 2007, in a story by Jodi Kantor discussing how Obama disinvited Wright from delivering the invocation.

"'Fifteen minutes before Shabbos [the Sabbath] I get a call from Barack," Wright told the *Times*. "One of his members had talked him into uninviting me," he said, referring to Obama's campaign advisers.

"You can get kind of rough in the sermons, so what we've decided is that it's best for you not to be out there in public," Obama told his old friend. The *Times* further reported that, according to Wright, Obama also brought up the *Rolling Stone* piece in that phone call.

The *Times* buried the story on page nineteen, leaving out all the inflammatory specifics about Wright's "rough sermons" that had already appeared in *Rolling Stone*.

The *Times* did note that "some say" the church's teachings "are overly Afrocentric to the point of excluding whites." And the story quoted an Obama spokesman as saying, "Senator Obama is proud of his pastor and his church, but because of the type of attention it was receiving on blogs and conservative talk shows, he decided to avoid having statements and beliefs being used out of context and forcing the entire church to defend itself."

On April 30, 2007, the *Times* ran a longer piece on the Wright-Obama connection, this one under the headline, "A candidate, His Minister and the Search for Faith." This story, also by Jodi Kantor, began on page one. It examined Obama's relationship with Wright in greater depth, and this time it made a number of references to Wright's radicalism, including a passing mention of his now infamous post-9/11 sermon. But Wright's radicalism was just one of many elements in the piece, not its focus.

"Mr. Obama was entranced by Mr. Wright, whose sermons fused analysis of the Bible with outrage at what he saw as the racism of everything from daily life in Chicago to American foreign policy," the *Times* reported.

And this is how the paper delicately touched on Wright's belief that the United States was not simply an innocent victim on September 11, 2001: "On the Sunday after the terrorist attacks of 9/11, Mr. Wright said the attacks were a consequence of violent American policies."

Well, that certainly is one way to put it, but it doesn't really capture the wild-eyed rant that Wright unleashed. Here's what Wright actually told his cheering congregation just five days after the 9/11 attacks: "We bombed Hiroshima, we bombed Nagasaki, and we nuked far more than the thousands in New York and the Pentagon, and we never batted an eye. We have supported state terrorism against the Palestinians and black South Africans, and now we are indignant because the stuff we have done overseas is now brought right back to our own front yards."

The story also left out Wright's conclusion: "America's chickens are coming home to roost."

•   •   •

As the campaign between Obama and Hillary Clinton heated up, Wright's inflammatory rhetoric about the contest drew increasing attention in the press.

On January 18, 2008, the *New York Post* reported, "The pastor whom Barack Obama calls his spiritual guide and mentor took a stunning shot at Bill Clinton this week, saying the ex-president did the same thing to black voters that "he did to Monica Lewinsky."

And Wright began getting some play on cable television too, especially on FOX News.

But the story didn't really heat up until March. That's when the tapes of Wright's sermons—yes, the same tapes the church had been openly selling to the public—finally surfaced.

Brian Ross first aired the Wright tapes on ABC's *Good Morning America* on March 13, 2008. Ross reported that "during the campaign the senator has defended what he calls Reverend Wright's social gospel." Then he played a soundbite of Obama discussing Wright's teachings: "So he was one of the leaders in calling for divestment from South Africa and some other issues like that. And he thinks it's important for us to focus on what's happening in Africa. And I agree with him on that."

Then Ross added, "But an ABC News review of more than a dozen sermons, which are offered for sale by the church, found Reverend Wright going far beyond issues of Africa. He refers to the U.S. as under the influence of the Ku Klux Klan."

After that, we heard the Reverend Wright himself preaching from the pulpit: "And they will not only attack you, if you try to point out what's going on in white America—U. S. of KKK–A."

A few days later the tapes showed up on FOX News, where they were played over and over again.

The *New York Times* also dealt with the growing firestorm. On page one? No. Try *page eighteen*. Again, the reporter was Jodi Kantor.

"Mr. Wright has been Mr. Obama's spiritual mentor," she reported, "and bloggers and television commentators spent the day picking over his stinging social and political critiques in the pulpit. It was not the first time that questions have been raised about Mr. Wright and his criticisms of the government (he has referred to it as the 'U.S. of K.K.K. A' for instance). But despite Mr. Obama's past attempts to distance himself from the harshest language, critics continued to question whether Mr. Wright's statements reflect Mr. Obama's beliefs."

But why was it left to "bloggers and television commentators" to "pick over" Wright's "stinging social and political critiques in the pulpit"? Wasn't that something mainstream reporters and editorial writers at big newspapers and television networks should have been doing all along?

On March 15, 2008, the *Times* ran—this time on page thirteen—its first detailed story about Wright's sermons (and then, only after Obama had raised the subject himself).

This time Jodi Kantor began her story, "In the handful of years Senator Barack Obama has spent in the national spotlight, his stance toward his pastor has gone from glowing praise to growing distance to—as of Friday—strong criticism. On Friday, Mr. Obama called a grab bag of statements by his longtime minister, the Rev. Jeremiah A. Wright Jr., 'inflammatory and appalling.'"

Of the Wright videotapes, Ms. Kantor wrote, "One of the statements that have been most replayed this week comes from the sermon Mr. Wright delivered following the Sept. 11 terrorist attacks. 'We have supported state terrorism against the Palestinians and black South Africans, and now we are indignant because the stuff we have done overseas is now brought right back to our own front yards,' he said. 'America's chickens are coming home to roost.'"

But by the time the *Times* and other major newspapers actually got around to quoting Wright's most provocative sermon, the whole world already knew what he had had said, thanks to the videotapes.

The point is this: if it had been up to the *Times*, we would never have known what Wright had said in that sermon—despite the fact that the church was selling the DVD of that very sermon. The paper only quoted from it after other outlets had made it into an international story that could no longer be ignored.

So much for "All the New that's Fit to Print."

• • •

As the firestorm that was fanned by the tapes continued to build—and Obama's candidacy seemed in genuine crisis—he gave his famous Philadelphia speech on race. For the *Times*, the speech not only put all questions about Wright to rest, but also confirmed that Obama was a healer and a visionary. The *Times* ran a "news analysis" of the speech on March 19, 2008, that read like a rave review written by the "Obama Girl." The author, Janny Scott, proclaimed that Obama's speech "may be the most significant public discussion of race in decades"; that "many historians said [it] could be likened only to speeches by presidents Lyndon B. Johnson, John F. Kennedy and Abraham Lincoln"; that it was "hopeful, patriotic, quintessentially American"; that Obama "confronted race head-on"; and that "historians and others described the speech's candidness on race as almost without precedent."

There, my friends, is your *Times* "analysis"—a glowing recap featuring quotes from a bunch of "historians and others" who adore Obama nearly as much as the *New York Times* does.

Then, of course, there was the *Times*'s editorial, "Mr. Obama's Profile in Courage." That title told you everything you needed to know about what was to come.

"There are moments increasingly rare in risk-abhorrent modern campaigns—when politicians are called upon to bare their fundamental beliefs," the *Times* intoned. "In the best of these moments, the speaker does not just salve the current political wound, but also illuminates larger, troubling issues that the nation is wrestling with.

"Inaugural addresses by Abraham Lincoln and Franklin D. Roosevelt come to mind, as does John F. Kennedy's 1960 speech on religion, with its enduring vision of the separation between church and state. Senator Barack Obama, who has not faced such tests of character this year, faced one on Tuesday. It is hard to imagine how he could have handled it better."

"On Tuesday," the editorial droned on, "Mr. Obama drew a bright line between his religious connection with Mr. Wright, which should be none of the voters' business, and having a political connection, which would be very much their business. The distinction seems especially urgent after seven years of a president who has worked to blur the line between church and state."

Nice touch: Praise Obama *and* bash Bush—both in the very same paragraph!

Then, from the high moral perch of their building, not far from the few remaining sex shops in Times Square, the wise men and women of the *New York Times* informed us that, "Mr. Obama's eloquent speech should end the debate over his ties to Mr. Wright."

Check please! The *New York Times* had just told all of us—and "us" includes all those journalists who hang on every syllable the *Times* prints—that we need no more talk, no more investigation, no more debate, *no more nothing* regarding the nexus between Wright and Obama. Now, with its editorial, it was official: any further criticism of Obama's relationship with Wright was old news, out of bounds, and most likely racist. In other word, this story was declared over, dead, and buried.

●   ●   ●

The lesson of the Jeremiah Wright story is this: if Obama could survive this, he could survive anything—and that the Obama-friendly media (again, consciously or otherwise) would do whatever it took to help him. No revelation was too shocking, no association too extreme, that Obama, and his media amen chorus, would not bury it, ignore it, or explain it away.

The Wright story was the ultimate test—once they got away with that, they could get away with anything.

Indeed, the Wright story became a kind of template— both for the Obama campaign and the media—for how to handle virtually any story potentially damaging to Obama: minimize it, praise Obama for his candor, claim all questions have been asked and answered, and attack those who persist in asking questions as over-the-top partisans.

By the end of the campaign, it would reach the point where having to explain or justify this or that revelation about Obama's past was no longer even necessary. By then a public that had initially been stunned by Wright's appalling sermons would no longer react to *any* revelation about the Sainted One with shock or outrage. Obama could have been caught on videotape in drag, marching next to Fidel Castro in a May Day parade in Havana, and the media, along with much of the public, would have shrugged it off as a "distraction" or a "smear" or as evidence of "racism."

At the end of the day, thanks largely to the New Media and *Rolling Stone*, we learned quite a lot about the alliance between Barack Obama and Jeremiah Wright. But the 2008 election revealed even more about the cozy relationship between Obama and the mainstream media, and how far major news outlets were willing to go to get their man into the White House.

• • •

On the FOX News program *Special Report with Brit Hume*, Charles Krauthammer captured the overall inanity of the media's reporting (or lack thereof) on the Reverend Wright: "For the mainstream media, it has gone beyond the point of lack of curiosity, a lack of questions, a lack of probing into Obama's associations in the past. It's that it has dropped a curtain over these associations and implied or claimed, as it said in the editorial page of the *New York Times*, that to probe into them, to question them, and to bring them up is to engage in a form of racism."

"That's what's so amazing," Krauthammer declared. "It's that when Obama is forced because of events to make a speech about race after it's discovered that he had been in the church for twenty years with a raving racist, he says 'I can no more disassociate myself from him than my poor grandmother.' The press says brilliant, Lincolnesque speech. Case closed. If you bring it up again, you're a racist.

"Six weeks later he renounces his first position and he breaks, in fact, with Wright and says he is beyond the pale. The press again says case closed, he's done it again. If you bring it up again, it's racist.

"An ad appears in North Carolina which associates Obama with Wright. It is denounced in the *Times* and elsewhere as racist, and that becomes accepted.

"We are looking at the most left-wing candidate with the most radical associations since Henry Wallace in 1948, and the press has ruled out as illegitimate any inquiries into this."

That's your free and unbiased media at work.

Chapter Nine

JOE THE DIRTY ROTTEN BASTARD

At times it seemed there was more investigative reporting on Joe the Plumber than on any story since Watergate.

The first bombshell: his real name wasn't Joe. It was Samuel. Joe was his middle name.

Get the Pulitzer ready.

Then the Associated Press dug deep and found out Joe the Plumber did not have a plumbing license. My God! Not that!!!

The *New York Times* went to a union hall in Ohio to get the lowdown. "An official at Local 50 of the plumber's union, based in Toledo, said Mr. Wurzelbacher does not hold a license," Larry Rohter and Liz Robbins wrote for one of the political blogs on the *Times*'s website. "He also has never served an apprenticeship and does not belong to the union," the story revealed.

He doesn't belong to the union? What kind of monster is this Joe, or Sam, or whatever the hell his real name is?

Bloomberg, the business news outlet, found more dirt on this public menace, reporting that "'Joe the plumber,' the Toledo, Ohio, man whose complaints about Barack Obama's tax plan were featured in the final presidential debate, owes the state of Ohio almost $1,200 in back income taxes."

The *Toledo Blade*, Joe the Plumber's hometown newspaper, wanted to know if Joe was even eligible to vote. "Questions were raised Thursday morning whether Mr. Wurzelbacher is a registered voter." Turns out, he was.

No, this was not a good year for American journalism, but "the absolute nadir came with Joe the Plumber," as Michael Malone put it in his piece for the ABC News website. "Middle America, even when they didn't agree with Joe, looked on in horror as the press took apart the private life of an average person who had the temerity to ask a tough question of a Presidential candidate. So much for the Standing Up for the Little Man, so much for speaking truth to power. So much for... all of those other catchphrases we journalists used to believe we lived by."

The media had to destroy Joe the Plumber for just one reason: he was going after *their* candidate.

So we're supposed to believe that stories about the Reverend Wright and Bill Ayers and ACORN were "distractions," but that news about Joe the Plumber's tax records (and Sarah Palin's skirts and blouses) were important?

Sure!

Chapter Ten

MASQUERADING
AS THE NEWS

My first job in journalism was with the Associated Press in New York City. I started there on June 4, 1967, four days out of college. Back then, the AP was a "just the facts ma'am" kind of news organization. Just straight, honest news with no opinions sprinkled between the lines. We sent our stories out to more than a thousand newspapers and probably an equal of number of radio and television stations. In those days, we were the gold standard of journalistic objectivity. We set the agenda for everybody else. If I had tried to slip even the subtlest editorial comment into one of my stories, some old grizzled editor would have kicked my rookie ass into next month.

Five years later, I was one of the *Boys on the Bus*, the title of Timothy Crouse's book on the 1972 presidential election. I had just started with CBS News and I was one of the producers covering the campaign of George McGovern.

Crouse starts his fine book with a description of how important the wire services—AP and UPI—were in those days. "Most newspapers do not have their own political reporters," he wrote, "and they depend on the wire-service men for all of their national political coverage. Even at newspapers that have large political staffs, the wire-services story almost always arrives first. So the wire services are influential beyond calculations." The only problem with wire services, he argued, was that they "are usually bland, dry and overly cautious. There is always an inverse proportion between the number of persons a reporter reaches and the amount he can say. The larger the audience the more inoffensive and inconclusive the article must be."

That was then.

Now the once bland, dry, and overly cautious AP not only tolerates commentary in its supposedly objective news stories, it actually wants it—to try to stay competitive with the New Media, mainly the Internet, where everything is edgy and has a point of view. The AP calls it "accountability journalism." If they called it what it really is, their credibility, carefully built up over 162 years, would be shot. Because what the AP really practices these days is rightfully called "opinion journalism."

"Some of the most eyebrow-raising stories this presidential election cycle have come from a surprising source: the stodgy old AP," wrote Jay Newton-Small in the *Washington Post*. "And this new boldness is threatening not only the AP's standing as a neutral arbiter of the news but also challenging its relationship with its owners, thousands of struggling U.S. newspapers that are coming to see the AP as a monster of their own creation."

Not all the AP's "edginess" during the campaign was aimed in one direction, however. There was a story head-lined, "Is Edwards Real or a Phony?" Another one declared that "Obama Walks Arrogance Line." And another appeared about "Slick Hillary."

Liberal bloggers were not happy with any of those.

But more typical was this dispatch on May 10, 2008, by AP reporter Charles Babington. "Presidential campaigns have destroyed many bright and capable politicians," he wrote. "But there's ample evidence that Obama is something special, a man who makes difficult tasks look easy, who seems to touch millions of diverse people with a message of hope that somehow doesn't sound Pollyannaish."

I worked with geezers who literally wore green eyeshades and garters on their shirtsleeves. I was twenty-two when I started at the AP, and am certain I brought the average age in the place down to 117. If I, or any other reporter, tried to write something as saccharine about a politician as Babington did, the next thing I would have been told to write by one of those old-school editors would have been my own obituary.

But as bad as that kind of journalism can be, out and out advocacy, in the guise of analysis, is worse. In October 2008, after Sarah Palin told a rally that Obama was "palling around with terrorists," (referring to his association with Bill Ayers and presumably Ayers' equally radical wife, Bernardine Dohrn), Douglass K. Daniel, another AP reporter, filed a dispatch asserting that her remark had a "racially tinged subtext."

How in the world, you may be asking, were Palin's comments "racially tinged"? Here's how, at least in the fevered imagination of Mr. Daniel: "Palin's words avoid repulsing voters with overt racism. But is there another subtext for creating the false image of a black presidential nominee 'palling around' with terrorists while assuring a predominantly white audience that he doesn't see their America?

"In a post-Sept. 11 America, terrorists are envisioned as dark-skinned radical Muslims, not the homegrown anarchists of Ayers' day 40 years ago."

There is a point where political psychoanalysis becomes insanity itself—and this is it.

But Mr. Daniel carried on. The "most troubling" aspect of the Republican campaign, he warned, was "how allowing racism to creep into the discussion serves McCain's purpose so well. As the fallout from Wright's sermons showed earlier this year, forcing Obama to abandon issues to talk about race leads to unresolved arguments about America's promise to treat all people equally."

This is not "accountability journalism." This is crap journalism.

"But in a world, and a Web, full of analysis, opinion and 'accountability journalism,' what's missing is a neutral referee," Jay Newton-Small smartly pointed out in that piece for the *Washington Post*. "Which is a bit like living in a world with a North Pole and a South Pole but no equator. If there's no one to set the standard, how will we know when we've crossed the line?"

In other words, what's been lost is journalistic integrity; and too many in the mainstream media, to their eternal discredit, don't even realize it's lost it.

Chapter Eleven

GIVE ME A BREAK, I WAS ONLY EIGHT YEARS OLD

O n February 21, 2008, the *New York Times* ran a major investigative piece on one of the leading presidential candidates. It was a long piece beginning on page one and continuing inside the paper.

Unfortunately, it was the wrong investigation about the wrong candidate's association with the wrong figure.

The piece was about John McCain's alleged sexual relationship with a much younger female lobbyist—and was quickly exposed as a shoddily sourced smear. Even the paper's own public editor slammed the story, saying that although it "raised one of the most toxic subjects in politics—sex—it offered readers no proof that McCain and [the lobbyist] had a romance."

The story the *Times* might have used its vast editorial resources to pursue was the connection between Barack Obama and Bill Ayers.

Being the mighty *New York Times*, perhaps they could have actually gotten some real answers from Obama, and maybe even from Ayers himself. But that's assuming they wanted any.

In early February 2008, though you wouldn't know it from reading the *Times* or other mainstream newspapers, the story of Obama's relationship with the former Weatherman terrorist had already surfaced and was starting to attract attention around the world. One of the earliest stories about the relationship appeared on February 3, 2008, in the London *Mail on Sunday*. It was a lengthy wrap-up from the campaign trail written by Peter Hitchens.

"So who really is this Obama who can reduce knees and brains to jelly," Hitchens asked, "whose books are read with reverence by normally pungent critics, and who, we are told, is the new JFK? I traveled to his home city, Chicago, to see if I could find out."

In Chicago, Hitchens found a familiar name on an old list of Obama's campaign contributors, from back when he was running for a seat in the Illinois Senate—a name that raised the writer's eyebrow.

"His list of contributions shows one for $200 from a certain William Ayers. Can this possibly be the same William Ayers, now a Chicago professor, who used to plant bombs in the Seventies and has said: I don't regret setting bombs. I feel we didn't do enough? His partner, Bernardine Dohrn, once declared war on the US government.

"It wouldn't be surprising. Those (like me) who know the Left-wing codes notice things about Obama that suggest he is far more radical than he would like us to know."

Six days later, a newspaper in South Africa picked up the story. And a week after that, the Obama-Ayers connection was news in Ireland. The *Irish Examiner* ran a story observing that "Mr Obama could face questions about his relationship with William Ayers, a former member of the radical group, the Weather Underground."

"Ayers donated $200 in 2001 to Mr. Obama's Illinois Senate campaign and served with Mr. Obama from 1999 to 2002 on the board of the Woods Fund, an anti-poverty group," the paper continued. "The Weather Underground carried out a series of bombings in the early 1970s— including the US Capitol and the Pentagon. While Ayers was never prosecuted for those attacks, he told the *New York Times* in an interview published on September 11, 2001, that: 'I don't regret setting bombs.'"

The next day the story hit the *Times* of London, which noted that "Obama could run into further difficulties over his relationship with William Ayers, a professor of education at the University of Illinois and former member of the Weather Underground, a left-wing terrorist group that planted bombs in the Capitol and the Pentagon in the 1970s."

On February 19, 2008, the story appeared in the United States in the now-defunct conservative paper, the *New York Sun*:

Senator Obama's ties to a former leader of the violent left-wing activist group the Weather Underground are drawing new scrutiny as he battles Senator Clinton for the Democratic presidential nomination.

...Reached at his office in Chicago yesterday, Mr. Ayers declined to comment on his relationship with Mr. Obama.

In a statement last night, a spokesman for the Obama campaign, William Burton, acknowledged the $200 contribution from Mr. Ayers, who he noted lived in Mr. Obama's state Senate district and was once an aide to Chicago Mayor Richard Daley. "Senator Obama strongly condemns the violent actions of the Weathermen group, as he does all acts of violence," Mr. Burton said. "But he was an eight-year-old child when Ayers and the Weathermen were active, and any attempt to connect Obama with events of almost 40 years ago is ridiculous."

This appears to be the first time the *he was only eight years old* defense came into play, or that *it all happened forty years ago*, or that it's *nothing more than politics as usual*, and a *distraction from serious issues*. It would not be the last time that Team Obama or its allies in the media employed that defense. Rather, it became the standard response of Obama's defenders—in an out of the media—whenever the issue of Bill Ayers came up.

On February 20, the Arkansas *Democrat-Gazette*, the Clintons' old hometown paper, reported that "Another

Chicago academic ally of Obama's is Professor William Ayers, a Weather Underground radical in the 1970s."

And two days after that Ben Smith wrote a piece about Ayers for *Politico*, the widely read political online newspaper. Now the cat was really out of the bag. From that day forward, the big mainstream media could no longer pretend that only Obama-hating right-wing nuts were interested in the Obama-Ayers connection.

Smith wrote, "In 1995, State Senator Alice Palmer introduced her chosen successor, Barack Obama, to a few of the district's influential liberals at the home of two well known figures on the local left: William Ayers and Bernardine Dohrn.

"While Ayers and Dohrn may be thought of in Hyde Park as local activists, they're better known nationally as two of the most notorious—and unrepentant—figures from the violent fringe of the 1960s anti-war movement.

" . . . Obama's connections to Ayers and Dohrn have been noted in some fleeting news coverage in the past. But the visit by Obama to their home—part of a campaign courtship—reflects more extensive interaction than has been previously reported."

On February 29, Sean Hannity at FOX News grabbed the story—and never let go. But despite "fleeting news coverage" and the piece in *Politico*, the mainstream media still showed virtually no interest in the story.

But on April 16, 2008, that all changed. That was the night of the Democratic presidential debate in Philadelphia, a debate that was broadcast nationwide on ABC. And that's when a major, mainstream journalist shattered the decorum of the evening by asking one of those impertinent questions reporters are not supposed to ask of The One.

George Stephanopoulos, a co-moderator of the debate, said to Obama, "[Ayers] never apologized for [the bombings]. And in fact, on 9/11, he was quoted in the *New York Times*, saying, 'I don't regret setting bombs. I feel we didn't do enough.'" Then, after noting that Obama's campaign had described Obama's relationship with Ayers as "friendly," Stephanopoulos pulled the pin on the grenade. "Can you explain that relationship for the voters and explain to Democrats why it won't be a problem?" he asked.

The next morning, the question about Ayers was on page one of the *New York Times* and every other big city newspaper in the country.

"Throughout the 90-minute debate," the *Times* reported, "Mr. Obama was placed on the defensive, explaining his association with his former pastor, the Rev. Jeremiah A. Wright Jr., as well as his connection to Bill Ayers, a Chicago supporter who was a member of the Weatherman Underground and is now a professor at the University of Illinois at Chicago."

Times media writer Alessandra Stanley had a piece about the debate in the paper that day, too:

> But there were...moments when she [Hillary Clinton] and Mr. Stephanopoulos seemed back to their old war room sync. Mr. Stephanopoulos asked Mr. Obama about his ties to Bill Ayers, the Weatherman who in the summer of 2001 said, "I don't regret setting bombs; I feel we didn't do enough."
>
> Mr. Obama looked a bit surprised, but deflected the question. "This kind of game," he

said, "in which anybody who I know, regardless
of how flimsy the relationship is, somehow their
ideas could be attributed to me—I think the
American people are smarter than that."

Mrs. Clinton took up where Mr. Stephanopoulos left off. "Well, I think that is a fair general
statement," she said, "but I also believe that Senator Obama served on a board with Mr. Ayers for
a period of time, the Woods Foundation, which
was a paid directorship position."

With the Ayers issue suddenly being addressed by both candidates at a major debate, one would think the mainstream
media would finally take an interest in the story. And they
did. But it wasn't Obama's ties to Bill Ayers that interested
them—it was *Stephanopoulos's ties to Sean Hannity*.

Stephanopoulos had been a guest on Hannity's radio
show just before the debate, and Hannity suggested that
Stephanopoulos ask Obama about his connection with
Ayers. The idea that a "right-wing talking head" would suggest a question to one of their guys—one who helped get Bill
Clinton elected president no less—was of far greater concern
to mainstream journalists than any connection Obama had
with an old terrorist.

Keith Olberman thundered, "The campaign may have
seemed dirty. It had nothing on one of the moderators of
the debate tonight. . . . The real story of this debate may not
be found where they found the answers, but where one of
the moderators found his questions: Sean Hannity of FOX
News."

Jason Linkins, a political reporter for the *Huffington Post*, alleged that Hannity had "spoon fed" the Ayers question to Stephanopoulos.

"The unseen influence of FOX News wormed its way into tonight's nominally ABC-hosted debate," Linkins wrote, "when Senator Barack Obama was asked to account for his tenuous connections to former Weather Underground leader William Ayers, who famously began a *New York Times* article with this statement: 'I don't regret setting bombs...I feel we didn't do enough.'

"The question was posed by George Stephanopoulos, who neither conceived of the question himself, nor disclosed the primary source of his donated inquiry: FOX News talking head Sean Hannity."

The *Los Angeles Times* reported that "ABC News' George Stephanopoulos...denied he'd been spoon-fed the question by FOX News host Sean Hannity."

Let's just call it The Obama Doctrine Regarding Out-of-Bounds Questions by Reporters Who Never Got the Memo about Out-of-Bounds Questions. The doctrine basically dictated that no probing questions about Bill Ayers would be tolerated. The subject was off limits. Such questions were simply dismissed as sleazy attacks from conservative big mouths and as pointless "distractions." And since Stephanopoulos is no conservative, the media sought out a link to a conservative—Sean Hannity—and accused *him* of being the evil genius behind the unconscionable Ayers question.

But they also needed to make an example out of Stephanopoulos, in case any other big name media figure got tempted to wander off the Obama reservation. And so they gave Stephanopoulos a good smackdown. Tom Shales of the *Washington Post* escaped from the psycho ward long enough to declare that Stephanopoulos during the debate "looked like an overly ambitious intern helping out at a sub-committee hearing, digging through notes for something smart-alecky and slimy."

The Pittsburgh Post-Gazette went even further and attacked Stephanopoulos' entire network in a story head-lined, "Sleazy as ABC: The debate that degraded."

And there's the media's narrative on the Bill Ayers story—it's a degrading story, and any renegade who brings it up will be slapped back into line.

•   •   •

Eventually, the Hannity–Stephanopoulos story faded away, and again the mainstream media largely ignored Ayers—until late August, when the *New York Times* discovered an angle it could genuinely get excited about: a nasty campaign by right-wingers to sandbag Obama.

"A new conservative group co-founded by a former cam-paign aide to Senator John McCain said Thursday that it would begin a major advertising campaign against Senator Barack Obama emphasizing his association with Bill Ayers, the 1960s radical and Weather Underground founder," the *Times* reported.

The *Times* also pointed out that a spokesman for the group "had worked for the Swift Boat Veterans for Truth, a group that ran advertisements against Senator John Kerry when he ran for president in 2004."

A day later, August 23, 2008, the *Times* had a follow-up. They finally began digging deep into the story—not the story of the Obama-Ayers relationship, but the story of who was behind the dastardly campaign to publicize this connection.

"The conservative group running advertisements that highlight Senator Barack Obama's association with the 1960s radical William Ayers is being financed by a Texas billionaire who has raised money for Senator John McCain and who also helped finance the Swift Boat Veterans for Truth campaign against Senator John Kerry in 2004."

Five days later the *Times* ran still another story, this one about Obama's counter-campaign to combat the ads.

"As Senator Obama's campaign makes its argument for his candidacy before a national audience here this week," the paper reported, "it is waging a separate, forceful campaign against a new conservative group running millions of dollars of ads linking him to the 1960s radical William Ayers Jr."

And while the mainstream media were downplaying stories about why Obama would have had *any* connection to an unrepentant terrorist, no matter how "flimsy," a quiet, unassuming scholar named Stanley Kurtz—who holds a Ph.D. in social anthropology, of all things—was doing the kind of reporting most journalists had shown no interest in doing. In pieces for *National Review Online* and in op-eds for the *Wall Street Journal*, Kurtz was connecting the dots between Obama and Ayers and uncovering all sorts of news we never saw in the mainstream media.

On September 23, 2008, Kurtz wrote in the *Journal*,

Despite having authored two autobiographies, Barack Obama has never written about his most important executive experience. From 1995 to 1999, he led an education foundation called the Chicago Annenberg Challenge (CAC), and remained on the board until 2001. The group poured more than $100 million into the hands of community organizers and radical education activists.

The CAC was the brainchild of Bill Ayers, a founder of the Weather Underground in the 1960s. Among other feats, Mr. Ayers and his cohorts bombed the Pentagon, and he has never expressed regret for his actions. Barack Obama's first run for the Illinois State Senate was launched at a 1995 gathering at Mr. Ayers's home.

The Obama campaign has struggled to downplay that association. Last April, Sen. Obama dismissed Mr. Ayers as just "a guy who lives in my neighborhood," and "not somebody who I exchange ideas with on a regular basis." Yet documents in the CAC archives make clear that Mr. Ayers and Mr. Obama were partners in the CAC.

If you got your news from Katie, Brian, or Charlie, as some 25 million Americans did each night, you would know absolutely nothing about this. If you read a big city newspaper other than the *Wall Street Journal*, you would not know about this either. The best journalism on why the

Obama-Ayers connection mattered was not even coming from a full-time working journalist, but from a guy whose field of expertise was *anthropology*. What the hell is wrong with this picture?

• • •

But if Obama's faithful fans in the mainstream media weren't paying attention to Stanley Kurtz, the Obama campaign was. And its operatives did not like what they were reading.

During the Democratic National Convention, Kurtz went on a local Chicago Radio Show hosted by Milt Rosenberg— and Obama supporters bombarded the station with complaints in a coordinated effort to silence both men. On September 18, 2008, the *Chicago Sun-Times* ran an editorial telling the Obama campaign to back off:

> It's startling to see that [Rosenberg's] radio show has become a target for an e-mail hazing from the Barack Obama campaign.
>
> Rosenberg's sin? Last month, Rosenberg had on Stanley Kurtz, a conservative writer exploring the connections between Obama and William Ayers, an education professor and former leader of the '60s radical bomb-making group, the Weather Underground.... Rosenberg's producer asked Obama officials to send a representative, and they declined.
>
> One e-mail from the Obama campaign on Kurtz's appearance urged supporters to tell WGN

that "they are legitimizing baseless attacks from a smear-merchant and lowering the standards of political discourse."

Tons of e-mails and phone calls from Obama fans poured into WGN.

We have no quarrel with the Obama campaign defending its candidate, but we see a stark difference between combating lies, distortions and spin—and shouting someone down.

The attacks on Rosenberg and Kurtz were coordinated by a campaign whose mantra encouraged us to put aside the divisive politics of the past. However, the irony was lost on the mainstream media, which showed no interest in the story.

• • •

Finally, in the last month of the campaign, the *Times* returned to the Obama-Ayers story, but only after McCain and (mostly) Palin began making it an issue on the campaign trail. And what did the *Times* investigation uncover? That Obama and Ayers did not have a "close" relationship and that their paths merely "crossed" while they worked in Chicago.

The *Times* story came out on Saturday, October 5. A day later, Sol Stern, a contributing editor at *City Journal*, published by the conservative Manhattan Institute think tank, noted that the *Times* referred to Ayers, a professor of education at the University of Illinois at Chicago, as a "school reformer."

"On *Meet the Press* Sunday morning," Stern wrote on the *City Journal* website, "Tom Brokaw...picked up this now conventional wisdom and described Ayers as 'a school reformer.' Calling Bill Ayers a school reformer is a bit like calling Joseph Stalin an agricultural reformer."

"At a November 2006 Education Forum in Caracas," Stern continued, "with President Hugo Chavez at his side, Ayers proclaimed his support for 'the profound education reforms under way here in Venezuela under the leadership of President Chavez. We share the belief that education is the motor-force of revolution...I look forward to seeing how you continue to overcome the failings of capitalist education as you seek to create something truly new and deeply humane.'"

And then Ayers, the "school reformer" as the *New York Times* and Tom Brokaw described him, raised his fist and shouted, *"Viva Presidente Chavez!"*

I'll bet you didn't know any of that either.

• • •

Throughout the campaign, Obama made it sound like his relationship with Ayers consisted of a chance meeting at Starbucks. And on the rare occasion when he actually had to answer a reporter's question about Ayers, Obama gave the standard, "I was eight years old when Ayers was planting bombs" reply.

True enough. But he wasn't eight years old in 1995 when he launched his political career at the home of Ayers and his "partner," Bernardine Dohrn, also a former Weatherman terrorist. And he wasn't eight in 2001 when Ayers said he didn't regret planting those bombs; that his only regret was that he "didn't do more."

Charles Krauthammer asked the salient questions that the mainstream media wouldn't: "Would you maintain friendly relations with an unrepentant terrorist? Would you even shake his hand? To ask why Obama does is perfectly legitimate and perfectly relevant to understanding what manner of man he is."

For Barack Obama the strategy was simple: just say "Bill Ayers [or anything else you don't want to talk about] is a distraction." Then, all Obama has to do is "count on his acolytes in the media to wage jihad against those who have the temerity to raise these questions," as the wise Mr. Krauthammer put it.

Journalists probably don't like to think of themselves as soldiers waging a holy war on behalf of a politician. But in 2008, that's exactly what they were.

Chapter Twelve

LIFE IN THE BUBBLE

Whenever I speak about bias in the news, the one point I make sure to drive home is this: contrary to what some conservatives think, there is no vast left-wing conspiracy to slant the news. Then I say I wish there were. That would be easier to deal with than what we have to put up with now.

Let me assure my conservative friends that Brian Williams does not show up at NBC News headquarters at Rockefeller Center in the morning, summon his top lieutenants, usher them into a little out-of-the-way room where he dims the lights and pulls the shades, and then, after everyone gives everyone else the secret handshake and salute, asks his journalistic comrades, *"How are we going to screw those conservatives today?"*

It just does not happen that way. Williams doesn't do it, and neither do Couric or Gibson. And in my day in network news, Dan Rather didn't do it, Tom Brokaw didn't do it, and Peter Jennings didn't do it.

The reason I wish the origin of the bias were so easily pinpointed is because if it were, nobody would tolerate it. Even liberals—the reasonable ones, anyway—would say, "You can't do that!"

The real problem is worse because, instead of emanating from some central source, the bias is ingrained throughout the fabric of the mainstream media, from top to bottom. It's worse because it is an *institutional* bias. The problem, in a word, is groupthink.

There simply are too many like-minded people in America's most important newsrooms, and like-mindedness has a way of reinforcing biases. So these journalists think that everything to the right of center is conservative, and everything to the left of center is middle of the road.

That's why journalism is so biased.

Statistics can be dull. But the ones I'm about to bombard you with explain better than anything else why the stories we got out of this last presidential campaign were so biased, and in a bigger sense, why mainstream journalism overall is so slanted.

Take a look at how journalists voted in several elections going back forty years, based on a wide variety of polls and studies:

- In 1968, 86 percent of journalists voted for the Democrat, Hubert Humphrey, over the Republican Richard Nixon
- In 1972, 81 percent of journalists voted for Democrat George McGovern over incumbent Richard Nixon
- In 1980, twice as many journalists voted for Jimmy Carter than for Ronald Reagan
- In 1984, 58 percent of journalists supported Democrat Walter Mondale, who lost to Ronald Reagan in the biggest landslide in presidential election history
- In 1988, White House correspondents from various major newspapers, television networks, magazines, and news services voted for Democrat Michael Dukakis over Republican George H.W. Bush by a ratio of 12 to 1
- In 1992, Washington bureau chiefs and congressional correspondents supported Bill Clinton over incumbent George Bush 89 percent to 9 percent
- In 2004, a poll of campaign journalists based *outside* of Washington, D.C., showed they supported the Democratic candidate, John Kerry, over the Republican George W. Bush by a ratio of 3 to 1. Those based *inside* the Beltway favored Kerry by a ratio of 12 to 1
- In 2008, a study by *Investor's Business Daily* put the campaign donation ratio of journalists at more than 11 to 1 in favor of Democrats

And how do journalists identify themselves in terms of liberal and conservative labels?

- In a 1981 study, 65 percent of journalists across the country identified themselves as liberals, 17 percent as conservatives
- In a 1996 study of journalists based in Washington, 61 percent said they were liberals, 9 percent said they were conservative
- In 2007 the Pew Research Center found there were four self-identified liberal journalists for every one conservative

And one final set of statistics—this one examining what journalists believe about a wide array of social issues:

- According to a major study conducted by the *Los Angeles Times* in 1985, a study of 2,700 journalists at 621 newspapers, 81 percent of journalists favor affirmative action in business and academia
- The same study found that 75 percent agreed that the "government should work to reduce the income gap between rich and poor"
- The *LA Times* also found that 57 percent of journalists said that America's disproportionate consumption of the world's natural resources was "immoral"
- In 1996, according to a Freedom Forum survey, 59 percent of journalists dismissed the Republican Party's Contract with America as "an election-year campaign ploy" while only 3 percent said it was "a serious reform proposal"

Yes, it is theoretically possible for journalists to be overwhelmingly liberal, and to overwhelmingly support Democratic candidates for president, and still be fair and objective in their journalism. But realistically, and in practice, there's no way. That liberal bias seeps into just about everything the media touch.

The problem is that life inside the liberal media bubble is too comfortable. It dulls the senses. It turns even well-educated journalists into narrow-minded provincial rubes. Inside the bubble, almost everybody thinks the same way on most of the big social issues of the day—whether it's gay marriage or abortion or racial preferences. Inside the bubble just about everybody believed that Obama deserved to win.

After a while, journalists inside the bubble don't even think they're taking sides or slanting the news. They think they're simply doing what's right. That is the seduction of the bubble. It lulls journalists into thinking that they really are fair and honest brokers of information.

That apparently is how Evan Thomas of *Newsweek* sees it.

"The mainstream media are prejudiced," he acknowledged in March 2008, "but not ideologically. The press's *real* bias is for conflict. . . . Inveterate gossips and snoops, journalists also share a yen for scandal, preferably sexual. But mostly they are looking for narratives that reveal something of character. It is the human drama that most compels our attention."

Bull!

If the mainstream media really were interested in character they would have wanted to know more about why Obama so much as had a cup of coffee with a man who wasn't sorry that he planted bombs at the Pentagon and the Capitol.

Nice try, Evan. But that's not how it played out during the campaign. Journalists weren't biased for *conflict*, they were biased for *Obama*, because he was a Democrat, a liberal, and an African-American.

"It is true that reporters are susceptible to flash and charm," Thomas conceded, "like most cynics, they are romantics in disguise. JFK and the early Bill Clinton were bound to get better press than insecure Richard Nixon or earnest Al Gore (who for some reason hides a raucous sense of humor). Right now," he wrote eight months before the election, "Obama and John McCain are popular with reporters. But if the usual laws of press physics apply, the media will turn on both men before Election Day."

Except it didn't turn out that way. The usual laws of press physics didn't quite operate the way Thomas told us they would. The mainstream media didn't turn on both men. They only turned on one.

And what Thomas didn't point out is that before the election, the media liked McCain mainly because he was not reliably conservative. They liked him not just because of the access he gave them on the Straight Talk Express, but because he would stick his thumb in some Republican eye then smile at his accomplishment. They liked him because he seemed to care more about what Teddy Kennedy and Russ Feingold thought than what conservatives in his own party thought. But as soon as their old pal McCain was going head to head with a liberal Democrat, the bloom was off the rose. That's when the usual laws of press physics hit him right in the mouth.

Chapter Thirteen

OR MAYBE IT DOES . . .

In late October, as the campaign was nearing the finish line, the *New York Times* ran profiles of the candidates' wives. One story had all the pathos of a Greek tragedy. The other was as sunny as *Happy Days*. Guess which was which.

In the profile of Mrs. McCain we discover that way back in 1982, when she was new in Washington, some unfriendly congressional wives didn't want to sit with her at one of their luncheons. It seems they liked John McCain's first wife better.

According to the *Times*, "Cindy McCain was new to Washington and not yet 30 when she arrived at a luncheon for Congressional spouses to discover a problem with her name tag.

"It read 'Carol McCain.' That was the well-liked wife John McCain had left to marry Cindy, to the disapproval of many in Washington.

"Fearing that the slight was intentional, she slinked to a half-empty table that never filled. 'No one wanted to sit at her table,' said Barbara Ross, a friend who was not surprised when Mrs. McCain announced a few months later that she was moving back to Arizona. 'It was like high school.'"

That is how the story began. And it went downhill from there.

We learn that Cindy McCain did not like Washington.

We learn that she worried about not fitting in.

We learn that from time to time her parents bought her gifts on behalf of her husband, who supposedly was too busy to buy them himself.

All of this raised some questions, asked by Byron York of *National Review*: "In what sense are these revelations, if true, newsworthy? And when you are doing a story about the wife of a candidate, do those big scoops justify the intrusiveness required to discover them?"

I have long thought that it would be a good idea to find some man or woman with oodles of money and start a foundation of sorts that would bring in gifted reporters and writers and assign them just one mission: to snoop into the lives of—(drum roll, please)—journalists!

These hired guns would nose around and then write hit pieces about some pathetic reporter who got stood up on prom night. They would dig into the life of an editor to find out why he got divorced. They would ask questions until they discovered why an attractive female columnist, for example, never got married. They would discover why a certain journalist had been in therapy for quite some time. They would do a story about why some writer was not popular with his neighbors. They would humiliate the poor journalists by running these "big scoops" in newspapers, websites, and on television networks.

Sounds like fun, doesn't it—reporters getting a taste of their own medicine? No, reporters aren't running for president, and they aren't even married to someone running for president. But journalists are important too, aren't they? They have special constitutional protections, don't they? And wouldn't it be nice to get the low-down on the people who bring us the news about everybody else? It might imbue these journalists with a bit of sensitivity next time they go out to try to unearth some titillating but useless information about, to use one example that comes to mind, the wife of a candidate running for president.

But I will put my fantasy on hold for the moment and continue with the *Times'* profile, which has still more grim information about Cindy McCain.

The *Times* reminds us that many years ago she was addicted to painkillers, a sad fact that was not exactly breaking news in October 2008, but what the heck.

The paper tells us she didn't like campaigning, that she was unhappy in Washington, that she felt lonely because she was the senator's wife and his staff "didn't really want to hang around with her," that "from the start, Mrs. McCain's marriage has been defined by her husband's ambitions," and that she has trouble telling the truth, or as the *Times* puts it, "In interviews some of Mrs. McCain's statements seem questionable."

Like what? Well the story lets us know she lied about going to Rwanda during the height of the genocide in 1994. Turns out she only went to the Rwanda-Zaire *border*, according to an aide to Mrs. McCain, "in order to assess the conditions of the refugees entering the country." And she didn't go *during* the genocide, but *after*.

Overall, the story is so dark and gloomy that you get depressed just reading the damn thing.

The McCain camp called the piece "gutter journalism at its worst," but that's the kind of reaction you would expect from the campaign.

Here's another response to the story: "The story about Cindy McCain was vicious. It looked for every negative thing they could find about her and it casts her in an extraordinarily negative light."

No, the McCain campaign didn't say that. A mainstream journalist did—Mark Halperin, the editor at large at *Time* and one of the magazine's top political analysts. Speaking at a forum in Los Angeles, Halperin noted that the *Times* article "didn't talk about [Cindy McCain's] work, for instance, as a mother for her children, and they cherry-picked every negative thing that's ever been written about her."

And what about the profile of Michelle Obama in the *Times*? Well, let's just say no one could fault you if you thought it was written by someone on her husband's campaign.

In fact, the profile quotes her husband's chief political strategist, David Axelrod, as saying Mrs. Obama "is very, very smart and sensitive."

It tells us that she addressed a rally in Akron, Ohio, and "had the crowd—a mix of a few thousand black and white voters—laughing and cheering throughout."

It informs us that Michelle Obama looked into the vast crowd and said, "So many precious little babies like that one!" after noticing one infant near the stage. "Just completely delicious!"

"The audience roared with delight," the *Times* reports. "And many clapped, too, when she said: 'I also come here as a mother; that is my primary title, mom in chief. My girls are the first thing I think about when I wake up in the morning and the last thing I think about when I go to bed. When people ask me how I'm doing, I say, 'I'm only as good as my most sad child.'"

As Halperin put it, the profile looked like "a front-page endorsement of what a great person Michelle Obama is."

On October 4, a few weeks before the profiles ran, the executive editor of the *Times*, Bill Keller, was part of a media panel discussion in New York, and was asked what he thought of the McCain campaign's earlier criticism of the *Times*, which you'll recall, ran that page one story hinting at an affair between McCain and a beautiful young lobbyist. "My first tendency when they do that," Keller said, "is to find the toughest McCain story we've got and put it on the front page, just to show them that they can't get away with it."

Maybe that doesn't explain the dark profile of McCain's wife on the front page of the *New York Times*. But then again, maybe it does.

Chapter Fourteen

PLANE-GATE

J ust a few days before the election, the Obama campaign threw three newspaper reporters under the bus, or more accurately, off the plane—the Obama press plane. We needed to make room for reporters from the candidates' hometown newspapers in Chicago, a campaign spokesman said. We also needed seats, he went on, for reporters from *Jet* and *Essence*, two glossy magazines aimed at African-Americans. The decision had absolutely nothing to do with politics, he insisted.

Because political operatives never lie, we must take him at his word. I'm sure it is nothing more than an odd coincidence that the three papers that got booted—the *Washington Times*, the *New York Post*, and the *Dallas Morning News*—all endorsed McCain for president.

The *Washington Times* ran a fuming editorial.

"For one thing," it said, "there is no getting around the fact that all three newspapers kicked off the plane just happened to endorse Mr. McCain. Moreover, Mr. Obama's supporters have been furious with *The* [Washington] *Times* when it publishes stories that are not favorable to their candidate. One was an Oct. 10 report by Barbara Slavin of *The Times* about Mr. Obama's efforts to delay signing an agreement with the United States on the status of U.S. forces in Iraq. Another was a piece by reporter Joseph Curl pointing to Mr. McCain's role in mobilizing support for the Iraq troop surge, which Mr. Obama opposed. Viewed in this context, the Obama campaign's decision to remove Miss [Christina] Bellantoni [the *Washington Times* reporter booted from the plane] smacks of being the latest effort by Mr. Obama and his supporters to retaliate against reporters that ask tough questions."

Nonsense, Obama's people said, it was simply a matter of supply and demand. There just were not enough seats for all the reporters who wanted to be there for the coronation...oops!...I mean the election.

The *Washington Times* wasn't buying it. This was part of a pattern, its editorial charged; a pattern of punishing journalists who would not fall into line.

"After Barbara West, a reporter on WFTV-TV in Orlando, had the temerity to ask some tough questions to Joe Biden, the Obama campaign cancelled an interview with Mr.

Biden's wife, Jill," the editorial stated. "Obama supporters even called for Miss West's ouster. After a reporter for KYW-TV in Philadelphia pressed Mr. Biden too forcefully on some matters, the Obama campaign said it would grant no more interviews to the station. When WGN Radio in Chicago announced it would interview Stanley Kurtz, author of several unflattering investigative pieces about Mr. Obama, supporters of the candidate flooded the station with telephone calls and e-mails demanding that Mr. Kurtz not be put on the air. It is a disturbing pattern. If this is how Mr. Obama acts as a candidate, how would he treat the press as president?"

That was an important question. Was this a glimpse of things to come? For Kirsten Powers, the liberal Democrat who worked for Bill Clinton before she became a political commentator, it was more like back to the future. In her *New York Post* column entitled "A Nixonesque Move by Team Obama," Powers asked another important question:

"This is bipartisanship?"

"The move," Powers argued, "is utterly at odds with a central part of Obama's message: the idea that he's a different kind of candidate—one who won't demonize opponents or critics, but will instead work hard to bring people together."

"But even Nixon," she noted, "didn't kick *The Washington Post* (which had broken the Watergate scandal) off the campaign plane."

What made the Obama campaign's explanation look especially lame was that it booted real journalists off the plane to make room not just for reporters from the *Chicago*

Tribune and *Chicago Sun-Times*, but for writers from glossies that run celebrity crap.

At the time the three newspapers got their walking papers, *Jet* ran a cover featuring a half-naked Toni Braxton with a tease about an interview that would explore the fascinating subject of her personal trials and tribulations. Meanwhile, inside *Essence* you could have read an "intimate interview [where]... megastar Beyoncé dishes on her new album, Jay-Z and life in the spotlight."

The *Washington Times*, the *New York Post*, and the *Dallas Morning News* got booted for *this*?

"Was the Obama move retaliation?" Powers wondered before answering her own question. "It seems unlikely. More likely, the campaign wanted to make room for fawning coverage—and who better to get rid of than papers that cover you critically?"

Because the expulsion might shed some light on an Obama presidency, I decided to see what the most important newspaper in the solar system, the *New York Times*, had to say about the matter. I checked every news story, every op-ed column, and every editorial, using the Lexis-Nexis database. To see everything I found, just turn the page.

No, you didn't miss anything. The newspaper of record ran absolutely nothing. So I did another search. This time I was looking for everything ABC, CBS, and NBC News ran. Turn the page to see what I found.

Correct! The networks did not run anything, either.

Look, I'm not saying Plane-Gate was the equivalent of Watergate. It was Obama's jet, after all, and he could let anyone he wanted on it, and kick anyone he wanted off it. No journalist has a constitutional right to a seat on the press plane and a bag of peanuts.

But that's not really the point.

The decision to boot reporters from less-than-friendly papers did not jibe with the image Obama had carefully cultivated throughout the campaign. He was "bipartisan," or even "post-partisan"—at least that's what his campaign kept telling us. And his loyal base—the national news media—kept repeating it. But this particular story didn't fit that template. And who knows, maybe if the story ever made it to the evening news, it might cause some of those voters who were still wavering to wonder just how post-partisan Saint Barack really was.

And the media wasn't about to let this silly airplane "misunderstanding" get in the way of the coronation. Did the mainstream media stand up for those three conservative newspapers? You don't even have to ask.

Chapter Fifteen

THE UNFAIRNESS DOCTRINE

Every now and then you hear something so outrageous that you think it's a joke. Except Charles Schumer, the senator from New York, wasn't kidding.

On November 4, 2008, Election Day, FOX News anchor Bill Hemmer was interviewing Schumer about the Fairness Doctrine, a subject of extreme concern to conservatives, who fear that if the doctrine ever came back to life it would rip out the heart of conservative talk radio, the one spot on the media landscape that conservatives dominate.

When Ronald Reagan became president, he said the Fairness Doctrine was stifling free speech on the airwaves and told the Federal Communications Commission to get rid of it. By 1987, it was gone. No longer would station managers have to balance out one controversial opinion with another—or face stiff fines and even loss of their broadcast license if they didn't. In 1982, while the Fairness Doctrine was still in place, there were about one hundred talk shows on radio. A decade later, when the Fairness Doctrine was just a bad memory, there were literally thousands on the air.

If the Fairness Doctrine were resurrected now, any radio station that ran, say, Rush Limbaugh or Sean Hannity or Glenn Beck or Laura Ingraham—or any other big, profitable conservative talk show—would have to make time for liberal shows. These almost certainly would get crummy ratings and bring in lousy revenues. So we can expect, with a new Fairness Doctrine, that stations will jettison a lot of conservative talk shows, especially the smaller ones, because they can't afford to take on money-losing liberal shows.

So on Election Day Hemmer asked Schumer a straightforward question: "Are you a supporter of telling radio stations in America what content they should have on their radio station?"

"Well, I think we should all try to be fair and balanced, don't you?" Schumer said, taking a potshot at the FOX News creed.

But radio is a private commercial enterprise, Hemmer pointed out. Is it the government's role to control its content?

"The very same people that don't want the Fairness Doctrine want the FCC to limit pornography on the air,"

Schumer replied. "I am for that. I think pornography should be limited. But you can't say government hands off in one area to a commercial enterprise but you're allowed to intervene in another. That's not consistent."

I am never surprised anymore when stupid people say stupid things. But Chuck Schumer got a perfect 1600 on his SATs and went to Harvard. And he actually believes that because the federal government is empowered to keep pornography off the airwaves, *to be consistent* it also has the duty to regulate political speech?

Never mind that old saying Harvard men probably know quite well—that consistency is the hobgoblin of small minds. Beyond that, it is breathtakingly obvious that there is a basic difference between CBS running a movie showing nineteen people having sex on the dining room table, and a radio or TV station running a serious discussion about the most important political issues of the day. Yes, technically both are a kind of "speech." But the two are so *fundamentally* different that it is difficult to take Schumer seriously.

Let's take him seriously anyway, however, just to see where the senator's passion for consistency leads.

According to those statistical surveys we discussed earlier, ABC, NBC, and CBS News all ran more negative stories during the campaign about McCain than they did about Obama. That doesn't sound fair. So, does Senator Schumer think a new Fairness Doctrine should force all those news organizations to balance things out? Or does he just want to control *conservative* news and information?

Remember when, during the campaign, Brian Williams, Katie Couric, and Charlie Gibson went to Europe with

Obama? You could make a case that their very presence gave the candidate more stature than he otherwise would have had. But they didn't go along with McCain when he went overseas. Does *that* sound fair, Senator Schumer? Would you like the federal government to force ABC, CBS, and NBC News to be fair?

Somehow, I doubt it.

•   •   •

Brian C. Anderson and Adam Thierer discussed the Fairness Doctrine in their book, *A Manifesto for Media Freedom*, which describes the very dark days that may lie ahead in our brave new media world. In their words,

> The Left has watched uneasily as power drains away daily from the CBS Newses and the *Time* magazines of the liberal mainstream media and flows toward a more politically pluralistic array of new media alternatives that range from (mostly) conservative talk radio to (Fox-dominated) cable news to the ceaselessly expanding (thoroughly bipartisan) Internet. And make no mistake: liberals want to snuff out this exciting, democratic world of analysis and debate and return to the good old days, when you got up in the morning with the *New York Times* and had dinner with Dan Rather—and basically kept quiet while your elite betters told you what to think....
>
> In its highest-profile effort to shut down the political speech it doesn't like, the Left is working

to restore the Fairness Doctrine or some kind of regulatory analogue. The effects would be seismic—nothing less than wiping out most political talk radio.

And they would not even need a debate or a vote in Congress to get a new Fairness Doctrine on the books. All it would take is the appointment of a new FCC chairman by President Obama. That would give liberals a three–to–two majority at the FCC, just enough to usher in the bad old days of government control over political speech on the airwaves.

As a candidate, Obama said he was not interested in pushing for a new Fairness Doctrine, not right away anyway. But Nancy Pelosi and a bunch of liberal Democrats in the Senate have already come out in favor of bringing back the odious doctrine. And if President Obama chooses not to get the ball rolling, they can do it—with a law that would stifle conservative talk on the airwaves—all in the name of fairness, of course.

I talked to *A Manifesto for Media Freedom* co-author Brian Anderson soon after the election about the likely effects of a new Fairness Doctrine. He explained, "If you were a station programmer and you had to balance a popular conservative show with a liberal show that no one was going to listen to, the economic model doesn't make sense. You're going to be losing money and you're going to shift formats, or certainly think about it. Rush Limbaugh would survive, because he gets a big enough audience, but smaller market shows, less widely syndicated shows—it would be a real problem."

Is it too simplistic to say that the real goal here is to crush conservative talk radio, I asked him.

Anderson didn't hesitate. "No, that's exactly the goal," he told me. "It would kill talk radio in general for the economic reason that liberals don't get sponsors on the air and don't get very many listeners. The example of Air America being the most recent failure. In New York, Air America at the end of its time on WLIB, which was its flagship station, was actually getting fewer listeners than the all-Caribbean format [that Air America had replaced]."

And that was with an extraordinary amount of favorable press, especially from the *New York Times*.

But it's more than the fate of talk radio that's at stake, Anderson warned. A new Fairness Doctrine would also deliver a major blow to the world of conservative *books*. "It would be a two-fer," he argued. "You would also get rid of conservative book publishing, because the number one way of selling conservative books is on conservative talk radio."

So the Fairness Doctrine isn't about balance at all. It's about nothing less than raw political power—the power to cleanse the landscape of "too many" troublesome conservative ideas. "Today's liberals are not in favor of free speech," Anderson told me. "They want power and control, not political debate."

• • •

With so much at stake, surely the mainstream media—the guardians of free speech in our society—would be all over Schumer's ridiculous comparison of porn and conservative speech. So I checked the news data bases, but all I could find were a few conservative commentaries. I could not find a single news story or editorial in any of the big liberal newspapers or on the television networks.

Imagine, though, how they would react if instead of Schumer, some bigshot right-wing Republican had said that, *in the name of consistency*, since the government has the power to step in and control porn on our airwaves, then it should also have the power to step in and control on-air *liberal* speech. Imagine the panicked editorials in the *New York Times* and *Washington Post* and *LA Times* warning of a new American fascism. But when it's *conservative* speech that is in the crosshairs, all they do is yawn.

As for Senator Schumer, frankly, I don't care if he really believes his outrageous nonsense about the importance of consistency. All I know for sure is that even smart guys with perfect SAT scores can be foolish. Consistency has nothing to do with any of this. Liberals want a new Fairness Doctrine for another reason altogether: they want to use it to crush the conservative opposition. Period.

Chapter Sixteen

NOW THEY TELL US

The day after the election, two heavy hitters from the media world went on the Charlie Rose show to inform us that Barack Obama is a slightly creepy, deeply manipulative guy.

Thanks for the information—*after* the election! The guests were Jon Meacham, editor of *Newsweek*, and Evan Thomas, its star writer and resident scholar.

Here is part of the exchange:

> **MEACHAM:** He's very elusive, Obama, which is fascinating for a man who's written two memoirs. At Grant Park he walks out with the family, and then they go away.

ROSE: Mmm...

MEACHAM: No adoring wife, no cute kid. He is the messenger.

THOMAS: There is a slightly creepy cult of personality about all this...

ROSE: Slightly. Creepy. Cult of personality.

THOMAS: Yes.

ROSE: What's slightly creepy about it?

THOMAS: It just makes me a little uneasy that he's so singular. He's clearly managing his own spectacle. He's a deeply manipulative guy....

THOMAS: He has the self-awareness to know that this creature he's designed isn't necessarily a real person...

ROSE: Ahhhhhh!

So let's review: two journalists who run one of the most influential national news magazines think Obama is "very elusive," "slightly creepy," "deeply manipulative," and not "necessarily a real person."

Was this some kind of April Fool's Day joke in November? After Obama gets elected, we're told by these two media hotshots who have been following the campaign closer than 99 percent of the population that they know less about the president-elect than they probably know about the doormen at their co-ops!

Ah, but there's more. Tom Brokaw had also appeared on Rose's show to inform us that he knew next to nothing about Obama. And he did this just a few days before the election. Obama had launched his campaign over a year and a half before, but apparently it took Brokaw until just before Election Day to decide that he had no idea who Obama was. Ain't journalism wonderful?

Here are a few snippets from that exchange:

ROSE: I don't know what Barack Obama's world-view is.

BROKAW: No, I don't either.

ROSE: I don't know how he really sees where China is.

BROKAW: We don't know a lot about Barack Obama and the universe of his thinking about foreign policy.

ROSE: I don't really know. And do we know anything about the people who are advising him?

BROKAW: You know that's an interesting question.

ROSE: He is principally known through his autobiography and through very aspirational [sic] speeches, two of them.

BROKAW: I don't know what books he's read.

ROSE: What do we know about the heroes of Barack Obama?

BROKAW: There's a lot about him we don't know.

Meacham, Thomas, and Brokaw are newsmen, right? It is their job to tell us who this Barack Obama is, right—and not run interference for him? It is their job to tell us how he thinks, what drives him, what he really believes in, right—and not hide their fears and suspicions until after they got him elected? And they wait almost until Election Day—or in the case of Meacham and Thomas, until *after* Election Day—to go on national television and tell us that Barack Obama is a creature created by Barack Obama who is not "necessarily a real person"?

Rush Limbaugh played the tapes from the Charlie Rose show then spoke for a lot of us:

> These guys are looking at Obama and they've seen him the exact way we have, all of this time. They only now, after they think they got him into office, are starting to talk about their fears, about how nobody knows anything about him; his resume is thin, he's only written two books, and they're autobiographies; we don't know what other books he's read.... We don't know anything about him. It's creepy, never seen a victory speech with nobody on stage.... Look at all that they refused to report. They had plenty of chances to write editorials at *Newsweek* magazine, and they didn't write one reflective of what they really saw and know and fear about Obama.

All of this raises an important question: *who the hell did we just elect president of the United States?*

Chapter Seventeen

IT IS WHAT IT IS

few days after the election, on November 7, two big players in the world of political journalism shared their views on the campaign at a seminar in Washington. I listened on C-SPAN, and what struck me was how cavalier they were about the media bias—how readily they accepted it as a simple fact of life.

Charlie Cook, a well-respected, long-time journalist who specializes in election forecasts and political trends, told the audience, "I think a lot of people in the news media were too young to cover Camelot and John Kennedy, they were too young in most cases to cover Bobby Kennedy and so I think they were star struck by this Obama phenomenon."

And how did their fascination with the celebrity in chief play out during the campaign?

"Let's face it," Cook said, "is there a Democratic and a liberal bias in the media? Of course there is. But they also love a good story. And the first African-American serious contender for the presidency was a great story. And a lot of people in the media absolutely loved it. I think you can say that the media had a finger, more than a finger, on the scale on the Democratic side."

The other journalist was Stuart Rothenberg who, like Charlie Cook, is an inside the Beltway political junkie. "I agree completely," Rothenberg affirmed. "I'm sure they [journalists] preferred Obama. They liked Obama. They're Democrats. Obama got better treatment."

Yes, Rothenberg and Cook were only stating the obvious—that the mainstream media wanted Obama to win. But then Rothenberg uttered a few more words that spoke to just how corrupt journalism had become.

"But, you know," he said, "it is what it is. It's the nature of the political environment.... Republicans ought to know that."

Then Cook chimed in, "As Stu said, it is what it is."

It is what it is? Five little words that constitute the grownup version of one little word that kids say when *they* don't give a crap: "*Whatever.*"

But were these two guys really so jaded that they were willing to write off this bias so dismissively? Were they really saying that Republicans have to understand how corrupt journalism is in the real world, and they just have to suck it up?

I couldn't get those words out of my head. *It is what it is.* Rothenberg and Cook, I figured, are the kind of guys who are always thinking about politics, the way most other guys are always thinking about sex. I wouldn't be surprised if they get turned on when someone calls them to leak the name of the guy who will be appointed as the official procurer of staples and pencil erasers in the West Wing. And yet these political mavens didn't understand what any middle school social studies teacher grasps: that in a country like ours we really do depend not just on a *free* press, but on a *fair* press.

But what really got me was how they just shrugged it off. *It is what it is.* Conscientious people don't say that about any other kind of bias. Conscientious people never said, "Sure, blacks have to sit in the back of the bus, but hey, it is what it is."

No, nothing is quite the same as race in America, so my analogy goes just so far. But I trust you get the point. It simply is not good enough to acknowledge bias then wave it away with an indifferent, "It is what it is."

This is why the bias problem persists. Because journalists haven't had the guts to stand up and say "'It is what it is' just won't cut it anymore."

But I'm not holding my breath that anything will change anytime soon. After all, they are who they are.

Chapter Eighteen

TEN QUESTIONS FOR BARACK OBAMA

I was trained as a reporter in the old school, the school of Murrow, if you want to call it that, which liberals profess to admire. If I had still been at CBS News during the campaign and had landed an interview with Barack Obama, I would have questioned him the old school way. Here are ten questions—and a few follow-ups—I would have asked him:

1. How do you define "post-partisan politics"—because it seems to me that what you really mean is "folks on the right, come over to the left?"

2. Name two or three conservative ideas you find use-
    ful and would be central to your "post-partisan"
    political philosophy.

3. Is it fair to say if Jeremiah Wright's sermons had
    not been made public you would still be worship-
    ping at his church?

4. What did your wife really mean when she said,
    referring to your candidacy, that it was the first
    time she was proud to be an American?

5. Some people believe that the reason so many
    young black people are behind the eight-ball in this
    country is *not* because of old-fashioned racism, but
    because of dysfunctional behavior: fifteen-year-old
    girls having babies, teenagers dropping out of high
    school for example. You spoke forcefully and elo-
    quently on Father's Day about this kind of behav-
    ior. But then you dropped the subject. As someone
    who enjoys tremendous support in the black com-
    munity, you might have had some positive impact
    on the lives of these kids if you had made it a recur-
    ring theme of your campaign. Why didn't you?

6. Regardless of your age at the time of Bill Ayers'
    bombings, why would you have anything—*any-
    thing*—to do with a man like Ayers, who not only
    planted bombs at the Pentagon and the Capitol,
    but who said his only regret was that he didn't do
    more to stop the war in Vietnam?

7. According to news reports, you have a half brother
    living in a hut in Kenya. Is that true? Have you ever

sent him money? If not, why not—since you've professed compassion for the poor?

8. You won't release your college records. That makes me wonder why not. Was it something you wrote while in college that you don't want voters to know about? Was it your grades? I'm puzzled, help me out.

9. How willing are you to disappoint liberals?

10. As you know, some critics have suggested the media went easy on you. Agree or disagree? What do you say to those who believe that journalists wanted to help shape history by doing what they could to get the first African-American elected president of the United States?

These aren't "gotcha" questions. For all we know, Obama might have good answers for them. But these are exactly the sort of questions the American people have a right to expect reporters to ask—and they were the very questions that were rarely, if ever, asked by the press on the campaign trail.

Why?

Because they didn't want to challenge their candidate; they wanted to help him win.

Chapter Nineteen

WHO BEAT JOHN MCCAIN?

A
s corrupt as the media were during the presidential campaign of 2008, the mainstream media did not defeat John McCain. They may have cost him a percentage point, but that's about it.

So what did contribute to his defeat? Let's start with history. Only one time since FDR-Truman have the American people elected the same party to the White House three times in a row (Reagan, Reagan, and Bush, 1980–1992). So going in, the odds were against McCain.

Then there was the financial meltdown. For a while, it looked like McCain had a chance of beating the historical odds, but after the economy tanked, so did McCain's slim chances of winning.

But mainly it was the Republicans who beat McCain.

When the GOP controlled both houses of Congress *and* the White House starting in 2000, Republicans spent money like the proverbial drunken sailor on shore leave. They thought they could buy their seats in the House and Senate if only they spent enough taxpayer money, and in trying to do so they discredited the entire party.

And how many outlandish spending bills did the "compassionate conservative" in the White House veto? Try none. In more ways than one, George Bush was an albatross around McCain's neck. He got the nation into an immensely unpopular war, and Americans don't like long wars. Whether the surge works in the long run or not, in 2008 voters were in a mood for change.

The voters saw how Republicans had sold out their principles. If they didn't stand for fiscal responsibility, if they got us into a war with no end in sight, if they kept telling us that they didn't believe in nation-building and then did just that in Iraq, then it was time for the new guy.

McCain also defeated himself. Let's face it, he may be a man of great character, but in the United States of Entertainment he just didn't make a good impression on television. When he was on a split screen with Obama, one of them looked like tomorrow, the other looked like yesterday. And the American people rarely vote for yesterday.

When Rush Limbaugh and Charles Krauthammer and Bill O'Reilly and Sean Hannity and Dick Morris and the editorial page of the *Wall Street Journal* make the case for

McCain better than McCain made it . . . hey, the guy deserved to lose.

And while Obama was breaking records raising money by harnessing the immense power of the Internet, McCain was flipping through his Rolodex trying to line up support.

As for his decision to put Sarah Palin on the ticket, she may have energized the Republican base, but the base was not enough to win the election. She had to energize the moderates and the independents. And she didn't do that.

Republicans have won in the past with the press rooting for the other guy. They might have won this time, too, even with mainstream journalists practically wearing Obama–for–President buttons.

But I suspect no Republican could have overcome such an unholy trinity made up of history, an economic collapse, and an unpopular Republican president in the White House. That was just too much.

Now Republicans have to take stock. They have to be introspective. They can't blame the media for all their problems. They have to admit their mistakes and figure out where to go from here, or they will continue to lose elections. The good news for the GOP is that they have some interesting thinkers in their ranks—people like Newt Gingrich and Michael Steele and a few governors like Haley Barbour of Mississippi, Bobby Jindal of Louisiana, and Tim Pawlenty of Minnesota. They will figure out, I think, how to regain the trust of the American people.

And that just happens to be the very same challenge facing the mainstream media. How will *they* regain the trust of the American people? History suggests they have a much bigger problem on their hands than do the Republicans. Politicians care what regular folks think, if for no other reason than they need regular folks to survive. The mainstream media don't give a damn what regular folks think. They haven't cared for years. Why change now, especially since their guy just won?

Chapter Twenty

WELCOME TO BAMALOT

A fter the election, NBC News said it was releasing a DVD entitled, *Yes We Can: The Barack Obama Story*.

ABC and *USA Today* announced they were coming out with a book about the election.

Time magazine ran a cover depicting Barack Obama as Franklin Delano Roosevelt, complete with FDR's signature cigarette holder.

Newsweek printed a cover comparing Obama to Lincoln. It also published a commemorative issue, "Obama's American Dream," which was "filled with so many iconic images

and such stirring prose it could have been campaign litera-
ture," as Howard Kurtz put it in the *Washington Post*.

The *New York Times* triumphantly declared that Obama
is the leader of a new generation—"Generation O."

New York magazine did a piece on "OBAMAISM,"
which it defined as "a kind of religion." But unlike, say,
conservative Christianity, this was a religion the mainstream media could like, because it is a religion "rooted in
a deep faith in rationality." It gets worse: "For those of us
born since World War II, never in our adult lifetimes (as
the next First Lady undoubtedly meant to say last winter)
has any single event made us prouder of our country.... We're all Dorothy, stunned at having just stepped
out—tripped out, one might even say—from a half-wrecked
black and white reality into a strange and glorious new
Technicolor world."

The *Chicago Tribune* trumpeted that Michelle Obama "is
poised to be the next Oprah and the next Jacqueline
Kennedy Onassis—combined!"

And our friends at MSNBC, Obama's official PR
machine, began running promos that announced, "Barack
Obama, America's 44th president. Watch as a leader renews
America's promise."

If they had a Clueless Hall of Fame, these slobbering
media ninnies would be charter members complete with big
dopey busts honoring their big dopey careers. For me, there
is something fascinating about how news organizations can
be so unaware of their sycophancy—a fancy word for ass-
kissing. Or maybe they're actually proud of their new careers
as press agents for Obama.

Howard Kurtz wrote about all of this in a piece head-lined, "A Giddy Sense of Boosterism."

"What's troubling here goes beyond the clanging of cash registers," he observes. "Media outlets have always tried to make a few bucks off the next big thing. The end-less campaign is over, and there's nothing wrong with the country pulling together, however briefly, behind its new leader. But we seem to have crossed a cultural line into mythmaking."

Welcome to Bamalot!

Kurtz also writes, "There is always a level of excitement when a new president is coming to town—new aides to pro-file, new policies to dissect, new family members to follow. But can anyone imagine this kind of media frenzy if John McCain had managed to win?"

"Obama's days of walking on water won't last indefi-nitely," Kurtz confidently predicts. "His chroniclers will need a new story line. And sometime after Jan. 20, they will wade back into reality."

Wanna bet?

• • •

After the election, Rachel Marsden, a conservative colum-nist, wrote a piece for *Human Events* about love, soul mates, and the media's undying devotion to Guess Who?

"Up until Barack Obama's victory, much of America—and the rest of the world—was deeply in love with the idea of being in love. The problem with any such relationship is always that, one day, the spell wears off, and you start get-ting annoyed at little things like your soul mate (in this case,

Barack Obama—America's soul mate) leaving the toilet seat up. Some media people won't care—they'll blame George Bush for having used the same bathroom months earlier. Others, like the mainstream media, will fall into Obama's toilet and splash around like it's holy water."

Let's just say my friend Rachel is not big on "dainty." So I asked her what she *really* expects from the press corps assigned to cover the Obama White House. Turns out, she had second thoughts after writing so unkindly about journalists splashing around in a toilet bowl. Unfortunately for them, her second thoughts were just as critical as her first.

"With Obama, the media will be like parents on the sideline at sports day," she told me. "Even if their kid turns out to be a dud, they'll still be defending him, because he's their baby: Barack O'Media. They'll have warm, tingly thoughts about the day they gave birth to him, and it will erase all the negative feelings associated with reality."

And while Rachel may be a tad snarky when it comes to the media, she's even got some mainstream reporters on her side. A print reporter I know who covered the Bush White House, and who says he voted for Obama, told me, "When there's a Republican in the White House, reporters see themselves as self-appointed prosecutors. But I'll bet not too many reporters are going to see themselves as prosecutors now that Barack Obama is in the White House. Who wants to prosecute Nelson Mandela? And trust me, Obama is closer to Mandela as far as reporters are concerned, than he is to some liberal Democrat like Dick Durbin."

Rush was right: Obama is too big, too important, too historically significant for the media to let him fail. While the media give every new president a honeymoon, this could be the honeymoon that never ends.

• • •

How can we expect journalists to scrutinize The One now that he's The One in the White House—after they worked so hard to get him elected?

How can we expect a reporter like Steve Osunsami of ABC News to report honestly on President Obama? On election night Osunsami went on the air, choked up, and came close to tears recalling how his "father used to tell us that there's no way this country would elect a black president," but "this evening, the country has proved my old man wrong—and we're the better for it."

I can appreciate the special meaning a black journalist attaches to the election of Obama, and indeed the special meaning his election holds for all African-Americans. But when a newsman says *"and we're the better for it,"* he crosses a very bright line between reporting and editorializing. And we have every right to question his ability to report impartially on a man he so admires.

But, let's face it: in 2008 these comments were nothing more than a *faux pas*, if that. After all, Osunsami wasn't exactly the only mainstream journalist who believed "we're better" for Obama's victory. Practically all of them believed it. Osunsami merely said it out loud, in public, on the air. At most, he was guilty of being a bit too candid.

So, I ask again: how can we expect journalists—black, white, brown, green, polka dot, or purple—to cover a man with whom they fell so madly in love during the campaign?

Let me take a crack at my own question.

Yes, there will be mainstream media reporters looking to establish themselves as "honest brokers" of the Obama presidency. The press, after all, went after Bill Clinton during the Lewinsky scandal (at least until he became a liberal martyr when the Republicans impeached him). But I think the reporting on President Obama will unfold in a special, protective context.

For example, journalists will remind us that he inherited a mess. If he cannot get done what he promised, or if his rate of progress is slow, or if he can't right the economic ship, there will always be a degree of understanding by his friends in the media—consciously or unconsciously, stated or implied. At times, this "understanding" will morph into outright undisguised compassion for the poor guy.

In his acceptance speech, Obama laid the groundwork. "The road ahead will be long," he told us. "Our climb will be steep. We may not get there in one year or even one term"— thus inoculating himself if he comes up short. And the mainstream media, I think, will carry that idea with them, because of the huge investment they made in his success. They will set up a construct in which all that turns out good will be to President Obama's credit. All that turns out bad will be Bush's fault.

In other words, heads Obama wins, tails Bush loses.

Although it's too late for the media to redeem its coverage of the 2008 election, they can still hold Obama accountable as president. They should closely examine his early actions in office, especially if he issues executive orders, and report promptly any of his decisions that may function as rewards for his campaign donors and other influential supporters.

I hope we don't have to wait too long to see those kinds of stories. But the media did work hard to get Obama elected, didn't they? So the question now is: will they risk undermining him in order to bring to the American people something as trivial as honest reporting?

Chapter Twenty-one

THE FIX

Here's my solution to the problem of media bias: diversity. What journalism needs is more diversity. And not just the kind we've grown accustomed to.

Journalism needs an affirmative action program for the smallest minority in America's newsrooms: conservatives.

I used to joke about this. But I'm not kidding anymore.

Once, just about everybody in the world of American journalism was white and male. So just about all the news we got came from that white, male perspective. It's not that those white males were bigots and would intentionally slant the news against women or African-Americans. It was just that white male journalists could not fully understand the subtleties of how black people saw the world, or how women saw it; about all the things they found important and interesting. And while we got some very good journalism in those days, we also got shoddy reporting riddled with blind spots.

For instance, in the old days the only time reporters and editors routinely noted a criminal's race in a news story was if the criminal were black. If a white guy robbed a liquor store, the story might read: "James Smith, a 25-year-old from Springfield, was arrested Saturday night after police say he held up a liquor store on Main Street."

But if a black man robbed the same liquor store, the story would almost certainly read: "James Smith, a 25-year-old Negro from Springfield . . ."

In retrospect, this strikes us as sheer racism. Why is the black man's race worth noting but not the race of the white man? But writing it off to overt racism, I think, is too simple an explanation. The sad fact is that's just the way it was back then. No one really thought about it all that much. But if there had been black men and women in the newsroom, the practice would have died long before it did. They would have noticed what those white male reporters and editors did not.

This is why diversity in our newsrooms makes sense. We need all sorts of perspectives to put out an honest newspaper or television newscast. But just what kind of diversity have we wound up with after all these years of trying to make things right? Well, we have white liberals and black liberals. We have male liberals and female liberals. We have gay liberals and straight liberals. We have Latino liberals and Asian liberals, too.

How nice.

What we desperately need now in America's newsrooms is *diversity of opinion*. News executives who have done everything short of setting up quotas to bring more women and minorities into journalism—and some have quietly done that, too—need to start hiring conservatives to cover the news.

It won't be hard. They can look for young journalists at conservative colleges, not just at the usual liberal places. Tim Russert, George Stephanopoulos, and Chris Matthews all moved from Democratic politics to the world of journalism. News executives can reach out to Republicans and help them make the same transition.

But please understand, I don't want these conservatives slanting the news to the right anymore than I want liberal journalists slanting it to the left. All most of us want is some fairness, and we think that diversity that goes beyond skin color and sex and ethnicity can provide it. Over the years we made sure that our newsrooms look like America. Now we need them to *think* a little more like America.

Who could argue with that?

ON THE ROAD
TO OBLIVION?

After Barack Obama won the election he found out the economy was worse than he thought; so he had to lay off seventeen journalists. (Rim shot!) The reason even liberals get that joke is because, like most humor that works, it has an air of believability about it.

How much of an air? Well, the Pew Research Center for the People and the Press asked registered voters a simple question: "Who do most reporters want to see win?"

Seventy percent answered, Obama. *Seventy percent*! Just nine percent said they thought the media favored McCain (and we can only hope they don't let these people have sharp objects). The rest said "neither" or "don't know."

When they broke the number down, Pew found that 90 percent of Republicans thought most journalists wanted Obama to win. Not exactly a breaking news bulletin.

But there was another number in the poll that should send shivers down the spine of any journalist with even half a brain: 62 percent of Democrats and independents also said the mainstream media were in the tank for Obama.

Nine out of ten Republicans think the media was rooting for Obama, and more than six out of ten Democrats and independents think the same thing. Or, to put it another way: just about *nobody* trusts these people to play fair!

Pew has been asking that same question since the 1992 Clinton-Bush-Perot presidential campaign, and while voters have always said the media favor Democrats over Republicans, the margins were never this wide before; the percentage of voters who think journalists are biased in favor of Democrats has never been higher.

But here's the real bad news: The mainstream media don't care about those poll numbers. They're riding high at the moment. They refuse to see the damage they are doing to themselves—and to the nation.

• • •

Less than a week before Election Day, on the FOX News program *Special Report with Brit Hume*, Fred Barnes said the same thing all those voters had told Pew: that bias was worse than ever this year.

"And you can see it particularly when there is a fundamental question that you ask about presidential candidates that the media are supposed to ask and then try to answer,"

Barnes argued. "And that [question] is: is this person running for president who he says he is?

"They have done it with John McCain. They say John
McCain in 2008 is not the guy we got to know in 2000. He is
a different guy running this year. We have heard that over
and over again.

"Now Barack Obama comes along, though, and here is
a guy who is presenting himself as someone who is bipartisan, bring us together, unify the country, change, hope.
And yet his political record is one of great partisanship, of
liberal ideology, being a part of a Chicago machine. And yet
the press has made no effort to square those things, to ask
questions about why we should believe Obama now and
what he says, because what he has done in the past is so
different."

Eventually, over the next four years, we will discover who
Obama really is. But wouldn't it have been useful if we had
a responsible media that asked the hard questions and
revealed the truth about this man, whatever it may be, *before*
he became the leader of our nation?

• • •

Back in 1972 when I was a young producer for CBS News
covering George McGovern's presidential campaign, Pat
Caddell, now a popular political analyst, was a young man
just out of Harvard who was doing polling for the candidate.

McGovern of course lost (he carried just one state, Massachusetts), and Nixon won a second term. We later learned
that Nixon had an enemies list. The youngest enemy on the
list was my old pal, Pat.

I ran into Pat at a political conference in Florida nine days after the 2008 election. I asked for his thoughts about the mainstream media.

They were more biased than ever, he said, before launching into a bit of history to put the current mess into perspective. "There is one institution in America which has no checks and balances," he told me. "And that is the press. And there was a reason for that. It wasn't that the Founding Fathers loved the press. It was because the press was supposed to protect the country. *That's* why Jefferson said, 'I would much rather have newspapers without a government than a government without newspapers.'

"But [when the media] leave the ramparts and become a partisan outrider for one party or the other or one candidate or the other; essentially [deciding] who should be president and who should not be president; what truth people should know and what truth they should not know; then what they become, what they constitute, is a threat to democracy."

"Why," he asked me, "should the American people support the First Amendment if the press isn't going to do its job for *them*."

And that's when this whole thing gets really scary.

Caddell worries that some day a demagogue is going to come along, somebody who makes Huey Long look like a shut-in. Somebody, Caddell told me, "who gets up at the start of his campaign and says, 'I want you to see the press. They are the enemy of the American people. They will do everything they can to stop me because they want to stop *you*.' And the American people will believe it. What if this is the most dangerous man that ever came along? Nobody will care what the press says."

And *that*, my friends, is why the corruption of the media matters. The press has constitutional protections for one main reason: to keep watch over a powerful government. The fundamental job of journalists is to look out for *us*—the American people! If nobody cares what the press says, journalists will be watchdogs in name only. They may bark from time to time, but nobody will listen. And their weakness will make it easy for a corrupt government to get away with murder. *That* is the danger we all face when the mainstream media go on a noble mission to make history. *That* is what can happen when the media, like that liberal professor at American University in Washington, believe that their role is not simply to report the news, fairly and accurately, but to *effect their kind of change in society*.

This time, they really screwed up!

Call it media activism, the journalistic equivalent of judicial activism. Just as judges are supposed to act as disinterested arbiters interpreting the law as it is written, so are journalists supposed to be disinterested *reporters* of the news, as well as interviewers prepared to grill Democrats and Republicans with equal relish. But just as judicial activists exploit their position on the bench to *make* law, so media activists exploit their position to shape the news. Instead of chronicling the news, they decide to influence it; instead of reporting on a presidential election, in 2008 they tried to determine its outcome.

There's no need to inflate journalists' egos, which are already the size of Mars, but we have to be aware of the danger when a nation no longer has trustworthy sources of information, when every media outlet is peddling a line, selling a candidate, promoting an ideology, acting as press officers for the favored (like Obama) and inquisitors of the unfavored (like Palin).

It's not just journalistic ethics that are at risk—democracy is.

•   •   •

The so-called mainstream media are dying a slow death. Circulation is down for many big newspapers. And TV network news ratings have been declining since cable and the Internet came along. So in large part, technology is doing the old media in. People read papers online these days; fewer and fewer buy the actual newspaper. More and more people get their news from cable television, rendering the old network news divisions less and less relevant.

The grim reaper is knocking on the mainstream media's door, and they remain gloriously oblivious. They have reached a tipping point but refuse to believe it. The corrosion that is eating away at their credibility has been happening slowly. It's like acid rain; one day you look around and all the trees are dead. Nobody pays attention until it's too late.

And when they become so irrelevant that no one listens to them anymore, they undoubtedly will lash out at their critics for poisoning the well. They will remain arrogant and clueless and blame the media bashers for damaging their standing with the public. But their demise won't come from the outside. It will be an inside job, the result of one too many self-inflicted wounds.

When that day comes it will be very bad indeed for the mainstream media. Pray, that their demise doesn't also lead to ours.

MEDIA ACTIVISM: A CASE STUDY

T he Media Research Center (MRC) did an extensive study of how the media shilled for Barack Obama from the time of his debut on the national stage up through his victory in the Democratic primaries. I reproduce the executive summary of the MRC's report here, with permission, as a case study of what "media activism" means.

OBAMA'S MARGIN OF VICTORY: THE MEDIA

How Barack Obama Could Not Have Won the Democratic Nomination Without ABC, CBS, and NBC

EXECUTIVE SUMMARY

It was the closest nomination contest in a generation, with just one-tenth of a percentage point—41,622 votes out of more than 35 million cast—separating Barack Obama from Hillary Clinton when the Democratic primaries ended in June. Obama's margin among elected delegates was almost as thin, just 51 to 48 percent.

But Barack Obama had a crucial advantage over his rivals this year: the support of the national media, especially the three broadcast networks. At every step of his national political career, network reporters showered the Illinois Senator with glowing media coverage, building him up as a political celebrity and exhibiting little interest in investigating his past associations or exploring the controversies that could have threatened his campaign.

These are the key findings of the Media Research Center's exhaustive analysis of ABC, CBS, and NBC evening news coverage of Barack Obama—every story, every soundbite, every mention—from his first appearance on a network broadcast in May 2000 through the end of the Democratic primaries in June 2008, a total of 1,365 stories. MRC analysts found that the networks' coverage—particularly prior to the formal start of Obama's presidential campaign—bordered on giddy celebration of a political "rock star" rather than objective newsgathering.

KEY FINDINGS:

- The three broadcast networks treated Obama to nearly seven times more good press than bad—462 positive stories (34% of the total), compared with only 70 stories (just 5%) that were critical.

- *NBC Nightly News* was the most lopsided, with 179 pro-Obama reports (37%), more than ten times the number of anti-Obama stories (17, or 3%). The *CBS Evening News* was nearly as skewed, with 156 stories spun in favor of Obama (38%), compared to a mere 21 anti-Obama reports (5%). ABC's *World News* was the least slanted, but still tilted roughly four-to-one in Obama's favor (127 stories to 32, or 27% to 7%).

- Barack Obama received his best press when it mattered most, as he debuted on the national scene. All of the networks lavished him with praise when he was keynote speaker at the 2004 Democratic Convention, and did not produce a single negative story about Obama (out of 81 total reports) prior to the start of his presidential campaign in early 2007.

- The networks downplayed or ignored major Obama gaffes and scandals. Obama's relationship with convicted influence peddler Tony Rezko was the subject of only two full reports (one each on ABC and NBC) and mentioned in just 15 other stories. CBS and NBC also initially downplayed controversial statements from Obama's longtime pastor Jeremiah Wright, but heavily praised Obama's March 18 speech on race relations.

- While Obama's worst media coverage came during the weeks leading up to the Pennsylvania primary on April 22, even then the networks offered two positive stories for every one that carried a negative spin (21% to 9%). Obama's best press of the year came after he won the North Carolina primary on May 6—after that, 43 percent of stories were favorable to Obama, compared to just one percent that were critical.

- The networks minimized Obama's liberal ideology, only referring to him as a "liberal" 14 times in four years. In contrast, reporters found twice as many occasions (29) to refer to Obama as either a "rock star," "rising star," or "superstar" during the same period.

- In covering the campaign, network reporters highlighted voters who offered favorable opinions about Obama. Of 147 average citizens who expressed an on-camera opinion about Obama, 114 (78%) were pro-Obama, compared to just 28 (19%) that had a negative view, with the remaining five offering a mixed opinion.

Perhaps if he had faced serious journalistic scrutiny instead of media cheerleading, Barack Obama might still have won his party's nomination. But the tremendously positive coverage that the networks bestowed upon his campaign was of incalculable value. The early celebrity coverage helped make Obama a nationally-known figure with a near-perfect media image. The protectiveness that reporters showed during the early primaries made it difficult for his rivals to effectively criticize him. And when it came to controversies such as the Wright affair, network reporters acted more as defenders than as journalists in an adversarial relationship. If the media did not actually win the Democratic nomination for Barack Obama, they surely made it a whole lot easier.

ACKNOWLEDGMENTS

I'm one of those authors who hates writing but loves having written. I have no peace when I'm writing a book. None! I'm always thinking about the next chapter or the next sentence or the next word. But the process is made much more bearable—and at times, actually enjoyable—when you work with editors who not only have a great deal of knowledge about the subject at hand, but also have big, smart, interesting ideas that make the book much better than it otherwise would have been.

So with a tip of the hat and a deep bow I express my gratitude to two of the best in the business—Harry Crocker III and Jack Langer at Regnery. They were, in a word, invaluable.

Thanks, too, to the creative folks who designed the unique, colorful, movie poster cover for this book—especially to Amanda Larsen and Chris Tobias.

And I am especially grateful for the friendship and encouragement of Marji Ross, my publisher, and Jeff Carneal, the president of Eagle Publishing, the parent company of Regnery, who not only got me started back in 2001 when they published my first book, *Bias*, but whose enthusiasm and support for this book made my job that much easier. They understand better than just about any mainstream reporter I know that the big journalistic issue that confronts us today is no longer simply media bias, but has become media activism.

My appreciation also goes out to my friends Harry Stein and Priscilla Turner for sharing their considerable knowledge on a wide array of topics that proved useful in putting this work together. Besides, it's always fun talking to them. Thanks also to the journalists who answered my many annoying questions; to Brian C. Anderson, who shared with me his considerable knowledge of the Fairness Doctrine; and to Pat Caddell, the political pollster turned pundit, whose wise observations appear in the final chapter of this book.

And a special thank you goes out to Rush Limbaugh, who graciously offered his time and considerable wisdom regarding the mainstream media, or the Drive Bys, as Rush puts it.

Then there's my longtime friend, Patricia Kopco.

Pat had absolutely nothing to do with this book. And I mean every letter of "absolutely" and "nothing." If Pat had insisted on helping even a little, I would have taken the easy way out and moved to Bangladesh. It seems, however, that I failed to acknowledge Pat in my last book (though I'm pretty sure she contributed absolutely nothing to that one as well), and I just learned that she pouted for several years afterward. That is something I can do without. An unhappy Pat Kopco is not a good thing—trust me on that. So I humbly offer a belated and most insincere nod to Patricia—as I say, for contributing nothing to this book. Thanks, Pat.

INDEX